THE GREAT AMERICAN CREDIT SECRET 3

The Great American Credit Secret 3

Antoine Sallis

Published by Game Changer Publishing

Paperback ISBN: 979-8-90158-034-9

Hardcover ISBN: 979-8-90158-035-6

Digital ISBN: 979-8-90158-036-3

GAME CHANGER
PUBLISHING
www.GameChangerPublishing.com

I would like to dedicate this book to my dad, Jessie Sallis.
For giving me inspiration and drive to never quit.

THE GREAT AMERICAN CREDIT SECRET 3

ANTOINE SALLIS

CONTENTS

How to Avoid the Flags That Route You Into the Danger Zone
AI watches more than you think. It listens to your patterns, studies your behaviors, and marks your inconsistencies. Learn how to move invisibly through the system.

How Banks Read Your Intent Before They Read Your Report
Your posture matters. Your patterns matter. Your digital fingerprints matter. Discover the subtle clues that separate high-limit winners from the ones who never leave the lobby.

The Unseen Currency That Opens Vaults Others Can't
Forget your score. What matters is your relationship. Loyalty, deposits, and trust form a second credit system. Master it, and you'll unlock doors that algorithms won't even show you.

How Artificial Intelligence Is Rewriting the Lending Game
You're not just being reviewed; you're being decoded. AI knows your patterns, your profession, your moves. This chapter reveals how to pass the machines watching the vault.

How to Live Like a Bank-Level Player Every Single Day
Some systems keep score in silence. Early warning systems. Fraud databases. Behavior flags. This is how you clear your name or never get flagged in the first place.

INTRODUCTION
YOU WERE NEVER
SUPPOSED TO SEE THIS

The doors shift. The vault hums. Your world tilts as you step into the quiet machinery of American finance. From this moment forward, you are not merely reading. You are entering.

You have just walked into the back office of the American financial system. Welcome. For now, I am going to be your secret friend who works at that bank. So I am about to tell you the exact inside information that most banks would prefer you never hear.

And as we begin, understand that walking through this doorway makes you part of the small group of people who finally get to hear the whispers, the unwritten laws, and the quiet truth that sits under the shiny lobby floors and marble countertops.

Starting here, know this clearly. **We need you to be approved.** We need you to open accounts. If we cannot lend money or hold yours, then the entire system collapses. Banks only get paid off the interest they lend, and they are allowed to lend against the deposits in their vaults. So lock this in as rule number one. **We need you.** And we need tons of people applying because we already know only a slice of them will qualify.

Once you understand that the whole machine survives only when people like you get approved, you will realize that you were never powerless; you were just never shown how to use the leverage you already had in your hands.

So yes, this is the true mindset of a lending institution. It is also one of The Great American Credit Secrets.

You ever wonder how someone with a perfect credit score gets denied while someone else with a shaky 690 walks out with a $25,000 approval? It happens constantly.

And if you have ever felt like something in the system did not add up, that quiet suspicion you felt was your intuition trying to tell you the rules are not what they look like on the surface.

You are not crazy for asking. You are just not on the inside yet.

That is what this book is about. Pulling back the curtain and giving you the same lens bankers use behind closed doors. Not the polished scripts from loan officers. Not the recycled advice from pretend financial gurus who never sat in a real underwriting meeting. I am talking about the actual rules, the ones they use inside the bank.

Because once you see how decisions are really made, you stop believing the surface-level explanations and start noticing the hidden moves that separate the insiders from everybody else.

Here is the truth.

Your public credit score is just the headline. But the banks are reading the entire story. And if your story does not match their secret script, you are getting declined, underfunded, or tossed into the dreaded manual review pile.

The deeper truth is that behind every approval or denial is a pattern the bank expects you to follow, and the moment you recognize that pattern, you start moving like someone who can see in the dark.

This book is Part 3 in a trilogy that exposes a blueprint the banks hope you never learn. But this one goes deeper than anything you have ever seen. You will learn:

- Why your real credit score is not the one you see in your app
- How underwriting actually works behind the scenes and how to glide past it
- What internal scorecards, AI systems, and fraud triggers banks use in 2025
- How to structure your profile to pull $100,000s or more in credit without breaking a sweat
- The Relationship Credit Loophole that turns loyalty into fast-track funding

You will meet people with bad scores getting approvals because they know how to play the game, and people with great scores getting denied because they do not.

And as you go through these stories, you will feel a shift in your thinking, because the more you understand the hidden mechanics, the more you start seeing opportunities where most people only see obstacles.

But the game has changed.

It is no longer just about chasing a number. Now it is about building a profile, telling a consistent story, and speaking the bank's secret language.

And once you learn that language, doors that used to slam shut suddenly open like they were waiting for you all along.

When you understand the system, you stop guessing.

You stop applying in the dark.

And you start moving like a true insider—calculated, strategic, and unshakable.

That is the shift that turns the average applicant into someone who walks into a bank with quiet confidence, knowing the outcome long before the underwriter taps their keyboard.

This is not financial advice.

This is financial warfare.

Let's get in the vault and use The Great American Credit Secret.

In other words, let's go **inside the bank.**

ONE
THE CREDIT CODE
CRACKING THE BANK'S HIDDEN FORMULA

The biggest lie in the credit world is the belief that your FICO score tells the whole story, when in reality, the bank has been reading a different book on you the entire time.

Most people really believe banks live and die by that number on their app. You check your FICO, you see a score, and you assume that's exactly what the lender sees, too.

But in reality, that little three-digit number is just one piece of a much bigger puzzle. I've been telling y'all this from day one. That's the whole reason this series even exists.

Behind the scenes, banks are running what I call the Credit Code. It's the internal formula that actually decides whether you get approved, denied, hit with a higher interest rate, or worst of all, get lowballed on a limit without even realizing it.

Here's the real key: your public credit score is not the bank's private scorecard. They're looking at way more data points than anything you'll ever see inside your Experian or Credit Karma app.

And once you understand that framework... once you finally see what they see... you can position your profile to pull approvals that most people don't even know are possible.

THE FOUR FACTORS BANKS WON'T ADVERTISE

Banks evaluate every applicant through four primary categories.

1. Capacity

Do you have the ability to handle the debt you are requesting? This goes beyond income. Lenders look at your cash flow, debt-to-income ratio, and even patterns in how you manage your monthly obligations.

Debt-to-income is the most important part of this category. You can make $120,000 a year on paper, but if your debt is too high, you still cannot afford much. One hundred and twenty thousand dollars per year is roughly $10,000 per month. If your rent is $4,000 and your car is $1,000, that is $5,000 out of $10,000 immediately. That is 50% before bills, food, clothes, subscriptions, childcare, medical expenses, or anything else.

Fifty percent DTI is way too high. Ideally, you want 25% or less. If a bank sees 50% DTI, your chance of approval goes down, your credit limits go down, and the only thing that usually goes up is your interest rate.

Remember this when you fill out an application. A smart rule of thumb is to use household or projected income. If you are married, have roommates, grown kids, or a partner sharing expenses, divide your rent amount legally and accurately. This instantly improves your DTI and increases your chances of approval.

2. Character

Do you demonstrate reliability? Your payment history, late payments, collections, overdrafts, and even how you have managed relationships with that specific bank all feed into this category.

This is why you want as close to zero negative items as possible. Always repair inaccuracies and remove outdated accounts. You can settle with lenders if needed, but always ask for deletion. The only phrase that matters is:

"If I pay, will you delete the account from my credit report?"

Anything else is a distraction. Phrases like "It won't hurt you anymore" or "We'll mark it as paid" do not mean deletion. That is just fancy language.

Another major factor is stability. Banks do not want to see sudden changes in your address, job, or phone number. That signals instability. Like I said in Part 1 of The Great American Credit Secret, keep your personal information the same as long as you realistically and legally can. If your mother has lived in her home for twenty years and you stay there from time to time, you can use that address. Banks value consistency more than anything because consistency means lower risk.

3. Collateral

If something goes wrong, what security does the bank have? Collateral is not always physical assets. It can include secured credit, guarantors, or any financial backing that lowers lender risk.

If you have great credit, you typically do not need collateral. This is where secured versus unsecured comes in. "Secured" means the bank can take something back, like a house or car. "Unsecured" means they trust your profile enough to give you money with no collateral at all.

Your goal is to build a profile strong enough to qualify for unsecured credit at low interest rates. Once you understand The Great American Credit Secret, you position yourself for high limits and prime-level rates. And when banks feel secure with you, two things usually happen.

They give you a high, respectable limit.

They give you a lower interest rate, often prime.

Prime is for clients with strong profiles. Subprime is for those who need improvement. Your mission is to sit on the prime side every time.

4. Conditions

External Factors That Affect Approval

Lenders do not make decisions in isolation. "Conditions" refers to the economic landscape around you. That includes national trends, interest rate shifts, government policies, and industry or regional risks.

Tariffs are a great example. When tariffs were introduced, entire industries were disrupted. Banks tightened lending to certain sectors not because the businesses had bad credit, but because the conditions made those industries riskier.

Now look at the AI boom.

Artificial intelligence has transformed the global economy and pushed billions of dollars into the United States. This affects you in two major ways:

First, that money flows into banks, SBA programs, credit unions, grants, and lending channels.

Second, any business even slightly connected to AI becomes more attractive to lenders because it is attached to a growing, well-funded sector.

That is how conditions either tighten or open the doors to funding. Right now, conditions are full of opportunity.

When the economy is strong, credit flows. When uncertainty hits, lenders tighten up. Rising interest rates make borrowing more expensive, and lenders become cautious. Lower rates make credit more accessible, but lenders look deeper at your stability.

Risk varies by industry, too. Real estate development, hospitality, and construction are viewed as volatile because they fluctuate with economic cycles. Banks often respond with tighter underwriting or higher rates.

Geography matters. If your business is in a region with high unemployment or economic decline, it can negatively impact how lenders view you, even if your personal financials are strong.

Here is the takeaway.

Before applying for business funding, research how your industry is perceived. If it is viewed as high risk, do not fight it. Pivot strategically. A small shift in positioning can change everything.

"Real estate investor" is high risk.

"Property management" is stable.

Same person. Same company. Different perception.

Your industry classification is determined by your NAICS code. Use tools like the Credit Genius App and ChatGPT to help you choose a code that accurately represents your work and positions you better with lenders.

A small shift in wording can open massive doors.

In essence, conditions shape the context of every credit decision. Even strong borrowers face resistance during economic downturns or volatile industry shifts. Understanding these external forces and timing your applications strategically gives you a major advantage and significantly increases your chances of approval.

THE SUBTLETIES THAT REALLY DECIDE OUTCOMES

Beyond these four categories, banks apply layers of nuance that rarely get discussed:

- **Account age** – Longer credit histories signal stability.
- **Utilization patterns** – Lenders don't just see what you owe today; they see how you've managed balances over time.
- **Internal behavior scores** – How you've treated *their* bank specifically matters as much as, if not more than, your external credit score.

- **Profitability models** – Some applicants are considered "too good." If you always pay balances in full and never generate fees, the bank may extend less credit than someone who appears more profitable.

WHY THIS MATTERS

When you understand the Credit Code, you stop relying on luck. You begin structuring your credit profile intentionally, the same way a business prepares a pitch deck for investors: every box checked, every red flag preemptively addressed, every number aligned with what the bank wants to see.

Approvals are no longer random. They become predictable. Denials become rare. And the conversation shifts from "Can I qualify?" to "How much can I qualify for?" These are facts.

The average person believes approval is emotional. They think it depends on the mood of the banker or if "the system is feeling generous" that day. In reality, it is math. It is algorithms and risk scoring. It is structure. When you understand that, you stop guessing and start engineering your credit outcome. That is how you become the architect of your approvals instead of a hopeful applicant.

The Credit Code helps you think like the underwriter. It teaches you how to shape your profile to match the lending criteria they use behind the scenes. When your profile speaks their language, you become easy to approve and hard to deny. That is what it means to be fundable.

Case Study: Jennifer vs. The "695 Approval Machine"

When banks evaluate a credit profile, most people assume the credit score is the beginning and the end of the story. Let us put that to the test.

Take Jennifer. She walked into the bank with an 800 credit score, which most people would call flawless. On paper, she should have been a dream client. But when she applied for funding, she was declined again and again.

Now compare her with another client. This woman had a 695 credit score, respectable but far from elite. Yet every time she applied, she walked away with approvals. High-limit credit cards. Lines of credit. Bank offers stacking up.

How can someone with a near-perfect score get denied, while someone with a good but not great score gets approvals everywhere?

This is the exact point. It is not just about the score.

Banks look beyond the three-digit number. They examine debt-to-income ratios, cash flow patterns, utilization history, internal bank behavior scores, and even how profitable you are as a client. Jennifer looked perfect on the surface, but her profile raised red flags once you dug deeper, such as imbalances, utilization issues, or account structuring that did not fit the bank's internal model.

Meanwhile, the 695 client had a clean, balanced profile that hit every checkbox lenders quietly prize: reasonable debt ratios, strong cash flow, stable history, and the right mix of accounts.

That simple contrast is the essence of The Great American Credit

Secret. The secret is not just chasing a number. It is learning to play by the hidden formula.

And that is where this book begins.

TWO
UNDERWRITING UNMASKED
WHAT UNDERWRITERS ACTUALLY DO AND HOW DECISIONS ARE REALLY MADE BEHIND THE SCENES

Most people imagine underwriting as a mysterious process where a faceless banker sits in a dark room stamping "Approved" or "Denied" on applications. The reality is more sophisticated and far more systematic.

And the deeper you look, the more you realize that underwriting is less about judging you and more about decoding the hidden signals in your financial life that reveal your true story.

Underwriters are not just individuals reviewing your credit. They are the gatekeepers of risk management. Their job is to ensure that every approval aligns with the bank's appetite for risk, regulatory requirements, and profit objectives. Think of them as the referees of the lending game, making sure the play is clean, fair, and beneficial to the institution.

And once you understand what these referees are really watching for, you gain the kind of quiet power that lets you shape your profile in a way that makes their decision feel almost automatic.

But keep in mind, sometimes underwriting is done manually by a set algorithm created by the lender, and other times it is an actual person reviewing your profile line by line.

And whether it is a machine scanning your data or a human looking into your financial history, the secret is that they are all trained to look for specific patterns that can either unlock your approval instantly or shut the whole thing down before you even hit "submit."

THE ROLE OF THE UNDERWRITER

At its core, underwriting answers one simple question: *Does this applicant represent an acceptable risk?*

To answer it, underwriters balance three critical lenses:

1. **Automated Systems** – The majority of applications first pass through automated underwriting software. These systems score your application against internal models in seconds. If you pass, approvals can be instant. If you fail, you're flagged for further review.
2. **Policy Adherence** – Underwriters are trained to apply the bank's policies, from minimum credit score thresholds to income documentation requirements. Even if you "feel" creditworthy, if you don't fit the policy box, you're likely out.
3. **Judgment Calls** – When the system can't decide, and in many institutions like credit unions, humans step in. This is where context matters: stable employment history, a strong banking relationship, or even the way supporting documents are presented can tip the scales.

BEHIND THE CURTAIN: WHAT THEY ACTUALLY REVIEW

Underwriters don't just look at your credit score. They review:

- **Credit Reports** – Payment history, utilization, collections, and derogatory marks.
- **Income Documentation** – Pay stubs, tax returns, or profit-and-loss statements for business owners.
- **Bank Statements** – Cash flow patterns, overdrafts, and average balances.
- **Employment Verification** – Stability of income, industry risk, and tenure.
- **Debt-to-Income Ratios (DTI)** – Ensuring your obligations don't exceed policy limits.
- **Collateral Valuations** (for secured loans) – Appraisals, assets, or property backing the request.

THE TWO PATHS: AUTOMATED VS. MANUAL REVIEW

1. Automated Review

Here is the insider truth: most banks want to avoid manual reviews completely. Manual underwriting is slow, expensive, and introduces human subjectivity. That is why banks build automated systems designed to handle as many approvals or declines as possible without ever touching a human desk.

If your profile fits the internal model cleanly, you get an instant or near-instant approval. The system scans your data, verifies your patterns, runs your scorecard, and greenlights you within minutes. This is the path you want.

2. *Manual Review*

If something does not line up, your application gets kicked over to a human underwriter. High utilization, inconsistent income, address mismatches, unstable employment history, or anything that looks suspicious can trigger this.

This is where most denials occur.

Humans ask questions that algorithms skip.

Humans dig into explanations that algorithms never care about.

Humans can say no even if the numbers look good.

Once your application hits a manual review queue, your odds drop sharply.

WHY KNOWING THIS MATTERS

Once you understand how underwriting really works, you stop applying blindly. You learn to engineer your entire profile so that it glides through the automated system without raising a single red flag.

When you pre-structure your data, align your income, stabilize your history, and match your patterns to what the algorithm expects, your approvals rise dramatically.

Automated underwriting is not random.

Manual underwriting is not personal.

Both are systems.

And when you know the system, you stop being at its mercy.

You become the architect of your own approvals.

UNDERWRITING AS RISK MANAGEMENT

At the end of the day, underwriting is nothing more than risk management. The underwriter's job isn't to judge you personally; it's to measure whether you represent a safe bet for the bank. And for you, as a borrower, the real game is learning what they look at so you can continuously position yourself for the best possible outcome.

Think of it like preparing for an exam you already know the questions to. If you know the test, you can study smarter. If you know the underwriting models, you can build your profile in a way that glides through approvals instead of getting stuck in manual review.

ALGORITHMS IN ACTION

Here is what most people never realize: underwriting is built on algorithms, not opinions. Behind the scenes, every tiny detail in your life and business is being fed into formulas that judge your stability, your credibility, and your risk level before a human ever sees your name.

These systems decide your fate long before you hit "submit." And once you understand how they think, you can bend the entire process in your favor.

Occupation Algorithms

Yes, your job title carries weight, and this is one of The Great American Credit Secrets. Certain occupations are coded as safe.

Engineers, nurses, educators, government workers, and long-term W2 professionals slide through scoring models easily because they represent consistency. We'll touch on this more later in the book.

Other roles trigger caution. Seasonal workers, high-turnover industries, gig workers, and contractors without paperwork are treated as unstable. And the biggest trap of all is checking the "self-employed" box without the documentation to back it up.

For the love of everything, do not put "self-employed" on applications unless your paperwork is airtight. To a bank's algorithm, that label might as well be a flashing warning sign. It is not personal. It is pattern recognition. Banks trust predictability, and if your occupation screams uncertainty, the algorithm will not hesitate to shut the door.

Business Credibility Algorithms

When it comes to business funding, the lender does not stop at your personal credit. They run a credibility scan on your company, too. They check your digital footprint like detectives checking a story for holes.

Do you have a professional website that actually looks real?

Do you have a business email, or are you still using Gmail?

Is your phone number consistent with online listings?

Does your business address look stable, or does it look like a P.O. box in disguise?

Do your records match across databases?

If your business looks polished, established, documented, and aligned across the internet, your approval odds jump dramatically. If it looks sloppy, outdated, or inconsistent, the system treats your company like a risk. It is not just about what you tell the bank. It is about what the internet tells them about you.

Lenders trust businesses that look like they are built to last.

These steps are simple, but they are powerful. One of the easiest ways to legitimize your business in the eyes of lenders is to establish your online presence, starting with a Google Business Profile. You can create one completely free. Just search "Google Business Profile," click the official link, enter your business name, upload your address, business hours, website, services, and logo, and then start collecting reviews from family, friends, or real clients. Once that is complete, your business now appears when a bank types your name into Google. You have a digital footprint, and that matters. To a lender, if your business cannot be found online, it might as well not exist. If it only exists on paper, it feels less credible.

Remember this. Banks and underwriters actually search your business on Google. They look for signs of legitimacy: website, reviews, address, phone number, and online presence. These elements help them feel confident that your business is real, active, and trustworthy.

Another critical element is your business address. A business address is almost like a business Social Security number. It is a personal identifier that carries weight. In fact, in consumer credit, someone can pull your score without even knowing your Social

Security number. All they need is your address and date of birth. That tells you how powerful an address is. That is also why, during credit repair, people often remove old or incorrect addresses before disputing items, because the address connects you to the account.

In business credit, your address works the same way. It builds identity and trust. Your business address should be consistent, professional, and tied to the business you are building. It helps establish that your company is real, active, and stable. It's even better if you happen to have an actual building with your logo splashed on the front in big bold letters, but ultimately, even a small office address is okay. This is one of the quiet foundations of The Great American Credit Secret.

PERSONAL RED FLAGS

Consistency is king in underwriting. Banks love stability because stability equals reduced risk. The moment your life looks inconsistent, you start triggering red flags.

- **Residential Stability**: Moving from place to place too often suggests instability. Staying at one address for several years suggests reliability.
- **Job Stability**: Frequent job changes, gaps in employment, or sudden shifts in industry raise questions. Long-term employment or steady career progression builds trust.
- **Mailing Consistency**: Using P.O. boxes or constantly switching banks creates suspicion. Lenders prefer a clean, continuous trail they can follow.

The big picture is simple: **underwriting rewards predictability.** If your personal life looks steady, your financial life looks trustworthy.

THE CREDIBILITY CHECK

Whether for personal credit or business credit, every application is quietly run through a credibility check. On the business side, that might mean scanning your website, your LinkedIn profile, your digital footprint, and how your company is registered with the state. On the personal side, it might include your job stability, your banking history, and whether your lifestyle presents as low risk.

This is not about perfection. It is about alignment. The more your story lines up across every touchpoint, the easier it is for banks to say yes, because you look like someone who fits the pattern of a stable, trustworthy borrower.

HOW TO STAY ALIGNED

The real takeaway is this: underwriting is not just about the numbers on your credit report. It is about the narrative your profile tells. Every decision you make becomes a chapter in that story. How long you stay at an address, how you move between jobs, how professionally your business presents itself online, and how consistent your financial habits appear all affect how lenders interpret your risk.

Your job is to manage the optics the way a business manages its brand. When you appear consistent, reliable, and profitable, lenders lean toward you. When you appear unstable or unpolished, they take a step back.

Once you understand that, everything changes. You stop playing defense. You stop being shocked by declines. You start shaping your profile so it glides straight through approvals because you are already speaking the same language the underwriters speak behind closed doors.

CLARIFICATION: IT IS ABOUT THE NARRATIVE, NOT THE JOB

Let's clear something up. There is absolutely nothing wrong with working at Walmart or any other company. But from an underwriting perspective, how you frame your occupation matters just as much as where you work.

If you are a supervisor or manager at Walmart, you should list "Supervisor" or "Manager" on your application instead of writing "Walmart." Titles tell a story. A leadership role signals responsibility, authority, and stability. A vague entry-level title does not create that same impression.

Underwriting is about connecting the dots. Your occupation, housing history, income, digital footprint, and credit behavior must all align into one believable, consistent narrative. If the story makes sense, underwriters lean toward approval. If the story raises questions or looks inconsistent, even a perfect score cannot protect you.

The lesson is simple.

Underwriting rewards alignment.

Your job is to present yourself in the most accurate and credible light possible, making sure every detail of your profile supports the same story of stability, consistency, and reliability.

THE NARRATIVE ALIGNMENT CHECKLIST

3 RULES TO KEEP YOUR STORY STRAIGHT

When it comes to underwriting, stability and consistency are everything.

Use this checklist before you apply for any funding.

Occupation Clarity

Always list your true role, not just the company you work for.

Titles like Supervisor, Manager, Analyst, Nurse, and Engineer carry more weight than vague or entry-level descriptions.

Your occupation should signal responsibility, maturity, and continuity. That alone can tip an approval in your favor.

Residential and Job Stability

Aim for at least two years at your current residence and two years at your current job whenever possible.

If you have moved or changed jobs recently, be prepared to provide explanations or extra documentation.

Avoid rapid changes right before applying. Multiple shifts in a short window raise silent questions you never hear but absolutely get judged for.

Credibility Across the Board

In personal credit: consistent addresses, steady employment, and no red flags like P.O. boxes or mismatched contact details.

In business credit: a professional website, a matching business phone number and email, and alignment across online directories.

The underwriter is connecting the dots. Every detail must support the same story of reliability and professionalism.

KEY TAKEAWAY

Your credit score is the headline.

Your narrative is the full story.

Underwriters do not sit there reading numbers. They follow the trail. They study the rhythm of your life, the silence between the data points, the way your history lines up or falls apart. Approvals are given to people whose story feels steady, believable, and built on real stability. When your narrative is aligned, the system leans toward you like it recognizes one of its own.

But if your story feels fractured or out of sync, it does not matter how high your score climbs. The algorithm senses the cracks, the underwriter sees the shadows, and the decision shifts against you long before you realize what happened.

In the vault, the story always speaks louder than the score.

THREE
THE SECRET SCORECARDS BANKS USE
THE CREDIT SCORE BANKS REALLY USE VS. THE ONE YOU SEE

The truth hits you like a cold gust when the vault door cracks open: the score you obsess over is not the score the bank is judging you by.

By now, you understand that banks don't rely **only** on the credit score you see on your apps. That three-digit number, whether it comes from Experian or even Credit Genius, is only the public score. It is designed to give you a general sense of credit health, but it is not the tool banks use to decide your fate.

Behind closed doors, lenders run internal scorecards, hidden formulas you will never see, and these often carry more weight than your public FICO or VantageScore. This is where the real game is played, the place where your approval is won or lost long before you hit the submit button. And now that you are here, we can finally show you how to step **inside the bank**.

Let's get it.

Now here is where things get even more interesting. Internal bank scorecards do not care about the story you tell yourself. They care about the story your entire profile tells them. They look at patterns, behavior, velocity, credit utilization trends, payment consistency, the age and depth of your history, and even the way your accounts interact with one another behind the scenes.

It is like walking into a nightclub where the bouncer already knows everything about you before you speak. You might think you are rocking an eight hundred in the public world, but inside the bank, your internal score could be something completely different.

And that is exactly why understanding this hidden layer gives you leverage, gives you power, and gives you clarity. We are not here just to teach you credit. We are here to teach you the psychology of approval so you walk through the financial system like you own the entire floor.

WHAT ARE INTERNAL BANK SCORECARDS?

Every bank builds its own proprietary scoring model. These aren't public, and they don't follow one universal standard. As a reminder, many times these scorecards play a much bigger role in the grand scheme of things. They are customized to predict one thing, so read this twice: "Will this customer pay us back and make us money while doing it?" That's it. That's the formula.

Where your FICO ranges from 300 to 850 on most scorecards (and some go up to 900), an internal score might range from 1 to 999 or A through F. You will never get to see the exact number, but it can determine whether you're offered $500 or $50,000. And here is where most people miss the secret sauce. Internal scorecards pick up on patterns you didn't even know you were creating. They watch your financial rhythm, how you treat your accounts during good months and bad months, whether you hover near your limits, how fast you open new lines, and even how predictable your financial behavior is. Think of it like having a backstage pass to your own concert. You might look composed on stage, but the bank is looking at everything happening behind the curtain. When you understand that, you stop playing the credit game randomly and start moving like someone who knows the house rules.

HOW INTERNAL SCORES DIFFER FROM PUBLIC SCORES

Here's what makes internal scores different from the consumer score you see:

- **Weighting** – Banks can decide which factors matter most. One lender may weigh income stability heavily, while another emphasizes how you've used their accounts in the past.
- **Behavioral Data** – Internal models don't just look at your credit report; they track how you behave with *their products*. Overdrafts, average balances, direct deposits, and transaction patterns all matter.
- **Profitability Models** – If you always pay your balances in full, you might look less profitable than someone who carries a balance and generates interest. That doesn't mean you'll be denied—it just means your limits may be lower.
- **Relationship Factors** – Length of time with the bank,

number of accounts, and even the depth of your deposits can boost your score internally.

- **Fraud & Risk Triggers** – Too many recent applications, mismatched addresses, or job instability can lower your internal score even if your public score is excellent.

WHY A 780 CAN LOSE, AND A 690 CAN WIN

This is where frustration kicks in. People say things like:

- "I had a 780 on Experian and still got denied."
- "My friend has a 690 and got approved for way more than me."

The reason is simple: **the bank isn't playing by the same score-card you're looking at.**

Your public score may look perfect, but your internal score could tell a completely different story, one shaped by stability, profitability, and risk. That's why someone with a lower consumer score but a rock-solid narrative (long-term job, steady residence, healthy banking history) can come out ahead of someone with a near-perfect number but weak stability signals.

WHY BANKS KEEP SCORECARDS SECRET

If you could see the exact formula, you could game the system. That is the only reason banks keep these models locked away. They treat them like intellectual property because these scorecards are competitive tools that help them decide who is profitable and who is risky. Every lender guards its internal scoring the same way a chef protects a signature recipe. They will let you taste the final result, but they will never show you the ingredients.

But here is the part most people do not realize. You do not need to see the formula to win. You only need to understand the inputs. Once you know what lenders value, you can start positioning yourself in a way that makes you look like their ideal customer. They want stability, they want consistency, and they want to know that lending to you will be profitable for them. If you can check those boxes with confidence, you can score high on any lender's hidden model without ever seeing your internal number.

Here is where the game gets powerful. Internal models track things beyond the basics. They look at the age of your accounts, your usage patterns, the way you manage limits, your risk behavior, and how predictable you are as a borrower. They look for signs that you panic or signs that you plan. They look for borrowers who treat credit like a business tool instead of an emergency button. When you understand that, you stop focusing on just getting approved and start focusing on looking like someone the bank wants a long-term relationship with. That is when your approvals get easier, your limits get higher, and your profile gets treated with more respect.

THE BIG TAKEAWAY

Your public score is the headline. The bank's internal scorecard is the story. Approvals, denials, and credit limits are all shaped by the story you're telling behind that number.

Once you understand this, you stop chasing points and start **engineering outcomes.** You'll know why a 690 can sometimes outperform a 780... and how to make sure you're always on the winning side of the hidden formula.

Next up, we'll dive into **The $100K Credit Profile Blueprint**, where I'll show you how to structure your credit to consistently qualify for the high-limit funding you deserve.

THE INTERBANKING CREDIT FACTOR

Now let's talk about something most people have never heard of, because I named it myself: **interbanking credit.**

This is the hidden score within the score. It's not about your FICO. It's not about what Experian says. Interbanking credit is how *your relationship with a specific bank or credit union* translates into lending power.

Here's how it works:

- **Number of Accounts** – The more accounts you have with a bank—checking, savings, credit card, loan—the more data they have on you, and the stronger your internal standing becomes.
- **Deposits & Balances** – Money talks. Keeping consistent balances or regular deposits builds credibility. It signals that you're not just a random applicant—you're a customer they profit from.
- **Length of Relationship** – Time is leverage. If you've been with a bank for five, ten, fifteen years, they're far more likely to extend funding than if you just opened an account last month.

- **Community Banking & Credit Unions** – This is where interbanking credit shines brightest. Even people with poor consumer scores often get $500 or $1,000 loans at credit unions simply because they've been members for years. That relationship can override the number on the credit report.

WHY INTERBANKING CREDIT MATTERS

This concept proves something critical: **relationships can beat numbers.**

Someone could have terrible credit on paper, but if they've banked with the same credit union for a decade, that history carries weight. On the flip side, someone with a perfect 800 score who just walked into a new bank yesterday is basically a stranger, and strangers don't get trust overnight.

This is why you should always think long-term when choosing where to bank. Every deposit, every account, every year you spend with an institution is building your interbanking credit in the background. And when the day comes that you need real funding, that invisible score can open doors your FICO alone never could.

KEY TAKEAWAY

Your **public score** gets you in the door.

Your **interbanking credit** decides how wide that door opens.

If you want approvals that stick, build the relationship just as much as you build the number. Stability, time, and loyalty are silent currencies in the banking world, and the sooner you understand that, the sooner you'll play the game on a higher level.

Case Study: The Power of Interbanking Credit

Let me show you exactly how interbanking credit works in the real world.

Take Marcus. Marcus has a 680 score, not bad but not excellent either. On paper, he is average. But Marcus has been banking with the same credit union for twelve years. He has a checking account, a savings account, and a small auto loan he paid off through them. His paycheck has been directly deposited there every two weeks for over a decade. The credit union knows his patterns, his balances, and his history. To them, Marcus is not just a credit score; he is a trusted member with years of proven loyalty.

When Marcus applied for a $5,000 personal loan, he was approved immediately. No questions. No manual review. That is interbanking credit in action. His relationship carried more weight than his FICO.

Now compare him to Samantha. Samantha walks into the same credit union with a shiny 780 score. On paper, she looks like a superstar. But she is brand new to the institution. She just opened an account last month. No deposits, no history, no ties. To the credit union, she is a stranger.

When she applies for the same $5,000 loan, she does not get the same treatment. Her application gets pushed into manual review. The underwriter asks for pay stubs, tax returns, and employment verification. She might still get approved, but the terms will not be as generous, and she will have to jump through hoops Marcus never even saw.

Here is what most people never understand. Banks care about risk and familiarity more than they care about the number on a screen. A long relationship lowers their risk because they have years of data that prove how you handle money. A new customer, even with a perfect score, is still untested. Interbanking credit turns loyalty into leverage. When you build a real relationship with your bank, you are not just a borrower; you are an asset. And assets get treated differently.

THE LESSON

This case study drives home the point:

- Marcus had a **lower score** but a **higher interbanking credit.** Result: easy approval.
- Samantha had a **higher score,** but **no relationship.** Result: slow approval, extra scrutiny.

The secret is simple: **banks trust history more than headlines.** Build your interbanking credit over time, and you'll unlock approvals and funding that outsiders can't touch.

FOUR
THE $100K CREDIT PROFILE BLUEPRINT

HOW TO STRUCTURE YOUR CREDIT TO CONSISTENTLY GET APPROVALS FOR HIGH-LIMIT FUNDING

Turn Your Credit Profile Into a Cash Machine

Up to this point, we have uncovered the hidden rules, the Credit Code, the underwriting process, and the secret scorecards banks use. Now it is time to shift from learning to executing. This is where everything you have absorbed turns into power you can use. In this chapter, you get a real blueprint, the kind that takes the mystery out of approvals and turns high-limit funding into something you can trigger with intention instead of luck. Once you understand how to position your profile the right way, lenders start viewing you as someone who can handle real capital, and the doors begin to open in a way most people never get to experience.

When I say $100,000 credit profile, I am not talking about one card with a six-figure limit. I am talking about a profile that is so strong and so well built that you can walk into multiple institutions and collect approvals like puzzle pieces. One bank gives you ten thousand, another gives you $25,000, another drops $15,000, and before you know it, you have stacked your way into six figures of available funding. This is the level where your credit stops being a score and starts becoming a tool. This is where your profile starts working for you, even when you are not in the room.

THE 5 BUILDING BLOCKS OF A $100K PROFILE

1. Strong Payment History

No late payments. Period. This is the foundation of every powerful credit profile. Even one recent late mark can knock you out of the running for high-limit approvals because lenders see it as a break in discipline. Think of your payment history like your financial reputation. You want it spotless, predictable, and dependable. Aim for twenty-four months of flawless payments before you start pulling high-limit funding sweeps. When lenders look at your report, you want them to immediately see consistency and control. Perfect payments tell the bank you handle credit with intention, and that sets you apart from the average borrower.

2. Optimized Utilization

Keep your revolving utilization under 10% for the best results. High balances signal risk even when your score looks great. Low balances show strategy, discipline, and stability. Lenders want to see that you manage credit, not that you depend on it. The lower the utilization, the more comfortable the bank feels approving larger limits. This single factor can upgrade your approvals from starter limits to real money that moves your entire profile forward.

3. Age of Accounts

A $100,000 credit profile needs depth. Ideally, you should have at least one account over five years old and an average age above three years. Age shows experience. It tells banks you have managed credit long enough to understand it. If your profile is young or thin, you can accelerate your growth with authorized-user tradelines or credit-builder accounts. Primary accounts hold the most weight, but authorized user lines still help create the depth and history lenders like to see while you build the rest of your profile the right way.

4. Thick Profile

Banks prefer a well-rounded credit file. Ten to fifteen well-managed accounts paint a picture of someone who understands how to handle different forms of credit. This includes revolving cards, installment loans, and even a mortgage or auto loan if you have one. A thin file with only two or three accounts becomes a red flag for high-limit lending. Think of it like walking into the ring with a beginner record. The more exposure you have across different account types, the stronger and more complete your approval profile becomes.

5. Interbanking Credit

Your relationship with specific banks matters more than most people realize. Interbanking credit is one of the most powerful advantages you can build. Multiple active accounts, regular deposits, and consistent activity inside a bank's ecosystem strengthen their trust in you. Trust turns into leverage. When you apply for higher limits at a bank you have been loyal to, they see history instead of risk. Build those relationships early, nurture them over time, and they will pay you back when you step up and request the larger limits most people can only dream of.

THE BLUEPRINT IN ACTION

Here's what a "funding-ready" profile looks like before you walk into a bank or apply online:

- **Credit Score Range**: 700+ (but with the right structure, 680s can still work).
- **Credit Card Utilization**: Under 10%, ideally under 5%. I don't recommend 0%; it's not a flex because it tells banks you don't use credit at all.
- **Accounts**: 10+ tradelines, with at least two major credit cards over 3 years old.
- **No Major Derogatories**: No bankruptcies, repos, or recent collections.
- **Stability Signals**: 2+ years on the job, 2+ years at the same residence, consistent addresses on file.
- **Banking Relationship**: At least one strong relationship account (checking/savings/credit card) with the institution you're applying through.

Case Study: The Blueprint at Work

David had a 720 score but only three open accounts, all less than two years old. On paper, it looked good, but it was not funding-ready. He applied for a business card and was declined outright. His profile had potential, but it lacked the maturity and depth lenders look for when approving serious limits.

Angela, on the other hand, had a 690 score but a layered profile with twelve open accounts, low utilization, seven years with her credit union, and a five-year-old major credit card. Even with the lower score, Angela walked away with $25,000 across two approvals in one week. Her history told a story of stability and control, and lenders responded to that long-term trust. She looked like someone who could handle money, and the banks rewarded her for it.

This is the power of the $100k Credit Profile Blueprint. It is not about chasing numbers. It is about building the right foundation so banks compete to lend to you. When your profile is structured correctly, lenders start seeing you as an asset **instead of an unknown risk. That is when the real approvals start showing up.**

KEY TAKEAWAY

A high-limit funding profile is **engineered, not accidental.** When you align payment history, utilization, account depth, and banking relationships, you create a structure banks can't ignore. Follow this blueprint, and stacking six figures in available credit becomes a predictable outcome instead of a lucky break.

EXPANDING THE $100K CREDIT PROFILE BLUEPRINT

When we talk about the $100k Blueprint, what we really mean is building all the pieces into your profile so that six-figure funding becomes achievable. It is about creating a structure that banks recognize instantly as low risk and high value. But here is the truth you have to remember. No two funding cycles are identical. Every round is influenced by your current utilization, the season the bank is in, underwriting shifts, internal scorecards, and even which lender is having a strong quarter. Sometimes you will walk out with $70,000. Other times, you might pull $120,000 or more on the first sweep. That range is normal because approvals depend on timing, the bank's internal appetite, and how well your profile is aligned at the moment you apply.

The beauty of this system is that you are not locked into one shot. In six to nine months, you can return and run the same strategy again, often pulling double or triple what you received the first time. Each cycle strengthens your profile, increases your banking relationships, and positions you for even larger approvals. The better you move, the more predictable your results become. It all comes down to how intentionally you build, how disciplined you stay, and how confidently you roll into each round with a profile designed to win.

THE FUNDING CYCLE STRATEGY

The most important rule is this: apply for everything all at once. When you enter a funding cycle, you do not stretch it out over weeks or even a long weekend. You move with precision and speed. A true funding run is a coordinated strike. Applications should be submitted back-to-back-to-back, whether you are going after personal credit cards, business credit cards, or lines of credit. You hit every target in one concentrated window. Why? Because inquiries and new accounts take time to update across the credit bureaus. There is a natural delay in the system. By the time lenders see the full picture, you have already secured your approvals and locked in your limits.

This is the strategy that allows people to walk away with six figures in funding in a single sweep. It is not magic. It is timing, structure, and execution. When you apply piecemeal, you give the bureaus time to report your new accounts, and you give lenders time to scrutinize your file. Suddenly, you start getting flagged for too many recent accounts or too many inquiries. Approvals slow down, limits shrink, and the entire cycle loses momentum. But when you move as a unit, you create a window where every lender sees you at your strongest. That synchronized approach keeps your profile clean in their eyes long enough to get everything you came for. This is how you turn one opportunity into a full stack of approvals instead of a handful of scattered attempts.

THE BUSINESS + PERSONAL COMBO

Another key to the blueprint is realizing you don't have to choose between business and personal funding: you can do both.

Let's say you go into a funding cycle with a well-structured business. On the **business side**, you may secure $60,000 in lines and cards. Then you immediately turn around and run the same strategy on the **personal side**, walking away with $70,000. Now you've stacked **$130,000 total** in available credit.

This is where people get it wrong: they chase one side only. But the real power comes from playing the mirror game, which is business and personal, side by side. Each reinforces the other, and your overall profile looks stronger every time.

THE MIRROR TECHNIQUE IN ACTION

You may remember this from *The Great American Credit Secret Part One*: the **mirror technique.**

The higher the limits already reporting on your profile, the higher the limits new banks are willing to give you. Lenders don't like being the first one to extend a big limit. But if they see that another bank already trusted you with $15,000 or $20,000, they're far more comfortable matching or exceeding that number.

That's why building your profile is like climbing steps. Once you secure one big limit, it opens the door for the next, and those approvals start to mirror each other. Before you know it, you're stacking $100,000 and beyond.

THE ROLE OF AUTO LOANS AND DTI

Here's a little-known piece of the blueprint: **having a car loan on your credit report can actually help.** Why? Because it shows you can handle installment debt responsibly, which banks like to see.

But there's a limit. Two car loans at once, or too much overall installment debt, and suddenly your **debt-to-income ratio (DTI)** tilts in the wrong direction. A high DTI makes you look overextended, and it kills high-limit approvals.

This is why the blueprint isn't just about adding accounts; it's about keeping your ratios in balance. **Low DTI + strong limits + diverse accounts = approvals.**

THE MIX THAT MATTERS

Banks like to see variety. A $100,000 profile isn't built on one type of account; it's built on a healthy mix:

- **Revolving Credit** – Credit cards with strong limits and low utilization.

- **Installment Loans** – Auto loans or personal loans with on-time history.
- **Business Accounts** – Credit lines, business cards, and vendor accounts that show you know how to leverage credit for growth.

Too many people ignore this. They focus only on their score or only on revolving credit and then wonder why their limits stall out. The mix is what proves to lenders that you're well-rounded and low risk.

PUTTING IT ALL TOGETHER

Here's the full picture:

1. Apply in a tight, back-to-back funding cycle so approvals land before new accounts update.
2. Stack both business and personal funding to maximize totals.
3. Use the mirror technique to let high limits breed higher limits.
4. Keep DTI in check—one auto loan is good, two is too many.
5. Build a balanced mix of credit so your profile tells a story of stability and diversity.

When you align these factors, six-figure approvals aren't luck. They're the natural result of a well-structured credit profile.

KEY TAKEAWAY

The $100k Credit Profile Blueprint is more than a formula. It is a strategy. The exact number you walk away with might vary—$70,000 this time, $120,000 the next—but once your profile is built to this standard, you will always be in the high-limit conversation. When your structure is solid, lenders look at you differently. You are no longer hoping for approval. You are positioning yourself for predictable outcomes.

Here is what truly separates the serious players from everyone else. People who chase credit are always reacting. They wait, they guess, and they hope. People who engineer credit create the environment for approvals before they ever apply. They understand the timing, the patterns, the bank relationships, and the profile metrics that influence every decision behind the scenes. And once you know how to engineer credit, you never go backward. You move with intention, you pull results on schedule, and you start treating credit like a tool instead of a scoreboard.

And that is the difference between chasing credit and engineering credit.

Case Studies: Running the Cycle vs. Dragging It Out

Let me give you a real-world scenario that shows exactly how the $100K Credit Profile Blueprint plays out.

Case 1: James Runs the Cycle Right

James had a 710 score, twelve open accounts, and low utilization. He followed the blueprint exactly as designed. When it came time to apply, he did it the right way, applications stacked back-to-back, all within the same cycle. On the business side, he secured $55,000 in lines and business cards. On the personal side, he locked in another $65,000 in revolving credit. By the time those new accounts reported, James was already sitting on $120,000 in fresh approvals. He succeeded because he moved quickly, leveraged his banking relationships, and used the mirror technique. Every new approval reinforced the next and created momentum across multiple lenders. His strategy turned his profile into a magnet for high limits.

Case 2: Daniel Drags It Out

Now compare that with Daniel. He had a higher score, a strong 750, but his approach lacked structure. Instead of applying all at once, he spread his applications out over several weeks. After the first round, new inquiries and accounts started reporting. By the time he went for his next set of applications, banks saw a spike in recent activity. That made him look unstable and unpredictable. The result was declines and low limit approvals, even though he had the better score on paper. At the end of his cycle, Daniel walked away with only $40,000. His profile was not the issue. His strategy was. And when the strategy is weak, the outcome always reflects it.

THE LESSON

These case studies make it crystal clear: **timing and execution matter as much as the profile itself.**

- James didn't have the higher score, but he had the better plan. He understood the power of stacking applications, mirroring high limits, and keeping his DTI balanced. The result: six figures.

- Daniel had the score but not the system. By dragging things out, he tripped risk alerts and left tens of thousands on the table.

The $100K Credit Profile Blueprint isn't just about having the right accounts... It's about **using them the right way at the right time.**

FIVE
THE 5-MINUTE RULE
HOW LENDERS SIZE YOU UP FAST

Here is the part nobody warns you about: the bank sizes you up long before they ever read your story.

Most people never realize that before a lender even digs into your file, they already know whether you are more likely to be approved or declined. Within the first five minutes, and often even faster, they scan quick-glance indicators that tell them if you are worth a deeper look or if you are already slipping toward a silent denial.

Think of it like the first impression in a job interview. You might have the perfect résumé, the qualifications, and the experience, but if you walk in sloppy or unprepared, the interviewer has already judged you before you speak.

Credit works the exact same way. The system forms an opinion before you even get a chance to defend yourself. And once that impression is set, everything that follows either becomes a confirmation or a contradiction of that first quiet judgment.

WHAT LENDERS LOOK FOR IN 5 MINUTES

When lenders do their "5-minute check," here are the things they glance at first:

1. **Score Range, Not the Exact Number**
   - They don't care if you're a 743 or a 751. They look at brackets: sub-prime, fair, good, excellent.
   - Once you're in the right bracket, the rest is structure and stability.

2. **Utilization Snapshot**
   - Are you maxed out on your revolving credit? If your balances are close to your limits, you instantly look risky, even if your score is high.
   - Under 30% is acceptable, under 10% is ideal.

3. **Derogatories and Red Flags**
   - Recent late payments, collections, or charge-offs jump off the page.
   - A clean record over the last twenty-four months signals reliability.

4. **Stability Signals**
   - Time at your current job, time at your residence, and address consistency are checked right away.
   - Frequent changes in either area are early warning signs for underwriters.

5. **Banking Relationship**
   - If you're applying where you already bank, they'll quickly glance at your account activity. Regular deposits and long-term history immediately boost confidence.

WHY THE FIRST IMPRESSION MATTERS

If you pass this 5-minute check, you move forward smoothly. If you fail, your application gets flagged for deeper manual review, and your approval odds drop dramatically.

This is why structuring your profile properly isn't just about the long game—it's about making sure the **first impression tells the right story.**

Case Study: The First Impression Flip

Lisa had a 735 score but was carrying 65% utilization on her credit cards. Within minutes of her application hitting the system, the algorithm flagged her as overextended. She was declined before an underwriter even had time to look at her strong income and stable job history.

Tony, on the other hand, had a 690 score but only 8% utilization, seven years at the same address, and consistent deposits with his bank. Within five minutes, the system tagged him as "low-risk." He walked out with a $15,000 approval.

THE KEY TAKEAWAY

The 5-Minute Rule proves one thing: lenders judge quickly. If your first impression checks the right boxes, you glide into approvals. If it doesn't, you get pushed into the manual review pile, where things get messy.

So before you ever apply, run your own 5-minute check. Look at your profile the way a bank would, and make sure it tells the story you want in that first glance.

BREAKING DOWN THE 5-MINUTE RULE IN DETAIL

When a bank or credit union receives your application, the system doesn't analyze every line of your report right away. It starts with what I call the **"snapshot test."** This snapshot is designed to answer one question fast: *Does this applicant look like a risk?*

Here's what that really means:

1. **Score Brackets, Not Perfection**
   - Lenders think in categories:
     - Subprime (below 640)
     - Fair (640–679)
     - Good (680–719)
     - Excellent (720+)
   - If you're sitting at 745, they don't see you as "better" than 735. You're in the same bracket. Stop obsessing over tiny point swings; instead, focus on stability in the range that matters.
2. **Utilization is the Fastest Red Flag**
   - This is one of the first data points a lender sees because it screams either discipline or desperation.
   - Over 50% utilization = desperation.
   - Under 30% = stable.
   - Under 10% = excellent.
   - Pro tip: Pay balances down 30–60 days before a funding cycle so the bureaus have time to update and show you in the best light.
3. **Derogatories = Stop Sign**
   - If your file shows recent collections, charge-offs, or late payments, the system throws up red flags instantly.

- Even if your score is strong, recent negatives can drop you into the manual review pile. That's why your first move before any funding play should always be cleaning up derogatories.

4. **Stability = Instant Trust**
   - Time on the job and time at your address get factored in right away.
   - Two years is the sweet spot. Less than six months? You look unstable, and your chances shrink.
   - Consistent addresses across your credit report also matter. Too many recent moves? Risk flagged.

5. **Banking Relationship = Secret Multiplier**
   - This is where the 5-minute check can flip in your favor. If you're applying through a bank you've been with for years, the system notes your direct deposits, balances, and overall behavior. That trust often overrides weaker areas in your profile.

HOW TO PASS THE 5-MINUTE CHECK EVERY TIME

Think of this like preparing for a job interview: you know the first impression will decide everything. Here's how to make sure your "snapshot" wins:

- **Clean the Negatives**: Handle any lates, collections, or charge-offs before a funding cycle.
- **Drop the Utilization**: Pay cards down under 10%. This one move alone can flip denials into approvals.
- **Stabilize Your Story**: Don't apply if you just switched jobs or addresses unless you absolutely have to. Give it time to season.

- **Leverage Relationships**: Apply first where you already bank. Then branch out. Banks like to take care of their own.
- **Think in Brackets**: Stop stressing over five-point shifts. Focus on landing solidly in the "good" or "excellent" bracket.

WHY THIS PAGE MATTERS

The 5-Minute Rule isn't just about awareness; it's about strategy. Once you understand the fast filters lenders use, you can design your profile to pass them automatically. And the moment you stop tripping red flags in those first five minutes, you stop living in the land of "maybe."

Approvals become consistent. Limits become higher. And the whole game starts tipping in your favor before an underwriter even knows your name.

Case Study: Winning (or Losing) the First Five Minutes

Case 1: Maria – Denied in Minutes

Maria had a 745 score and felt confident walking into her bank to apply for a personal loan. On paper, she thought she looked great. But here's what the underwriter's system saw in the first five minutes:

- **Utilization**: 62% on her credit cards.
- **Recent Derogatory**: A 90-day late payment from eight months ago.
- **Job Stability**: Three months at her new job.

That snapshot told the system everything it needed. Risk was flagged instantly. Maria's application was declined before anyone bothered to review her strong salary or her savings account balance.

Case 2: David – Approved Instantly

Now let's look at David. His score was lower than Maria's, only 702. But his five-minute profile looked clean:

- **Utilization**: 6% across three cards.
- **No Derogatories**: Two years of flawless payment history.
- **Stability**: Same address for five years, same job for seven.
- **Banking Relationship**: Checking and savings with the same bank for a decade.

The system read his file and saw stability, consistency, and low risk. Within minutes, David walked out with a $25,000 approval despite having a lower score than Maria.

THE TAKEAWAY

Maria had the higher score, but her 5-minute profile was messy. David had the lower score, but his story was airtight.

That's the power of the **5-Minute Rule.** Lenders aren't judging perfection; they're judging **risk signals at a glance.** Clean those up, and you'll pass the test before the clock even runs out.

AFTERTHOUGHT: FIRST IMPRESSIONS DECIDE THE MONEY

Here's the part nobody tells you: in 2025, lending is moving faster than ever. Banks, fintechs, and credit unions are relying heavily on **AI-driven underwriting systems**. That means your application doesn't just sit on a desk; it runs through algorithms that flag green or red in seconds. By the time a human underwriter ever touches it, the decision is already leaning one way or the other.

And here's the kicker: **the first impression is permanent.** If the system decides you look risky in those first five minutes, it takes a lot to turn that around. But if you look solid at a glance, you're already winning before the real review even begins.

REAL-WORLD ILLUSTRATIONS IN 2025

- **Fintech Quick Approvals**: Think about apps like *Apple Card* or *Chase MyLoan*. People apply and get an answer in 30 seconds. Nobody dug into your 40-page history— your approval or denial was made entirely off your **snapshot profile.** If your utilization was high that day, or you had too many inquiries in the past week, you were out.
- **Auto Loans in Seconds**: Car dealerships in 2025 now integrate AI credit engines. You fill out a form, and in less than two minutes, you've got a decision. Customers with "perfect" 780s but high balances are getting declined on the spot, while others in the high 600s with clean, low-utilization files are driving off the lot with new cars.
- **Business Credit Fast-Tracks**: Credit unions and regional banks now compete by advertising "instant

business lines up to $50K." But who gets them? Not the guy with an 810 score and five recent address changes. It's the business owner with a 690 but steady deposits for years, consistent EIN filings, and no recent negatives.

THE JUICY TRUTH

You cannot fake stability. You cannot walk into 2025 funding cycles thinking your "perfect" score is enough. The system is not impressed by numbers alone. It is studying your consistency, your utilization, your history, and whether your entire story feels believable from the very first glance.

Here is the real truth. Approvals in 2025 are less about your score and more about your signal. Your signal is the first five minutes of data that whispers to the algorithm and the underwriter: "This person is reliable," "This person is steady," "This person is profitable."

Get your signal right, and you can unlock six figures in approvals without breaking a sweat.

Ignore it, and you will sit there confused, watching someone with a lower score walk away with the funding you thought belonged to you.

And the part nobody tells you is this.

The system does not reward the loudest number.

It rewards the quiet stability hiding underneath it.

Master your signal, and the vault opens.

Miss it, and the door closes before you even realize it was unlocked.

SIX

THE "NO MANUAL REVIEW" GAME

HOW TO BYPASS THE RED FLAGS THAT TRIGGER HUMAN REVIEW

Here's a hard truth: once your application gets kicked into manual review, your approval odds drop fast. Why? Because humans second-guess. They see things algorithms overlook, and they dig deeper into areas you'd rather not highlight.

Banks would rather avoid manual review, too. It slows down the process, costs them money, and introduces subjectivity. That's why the smartest borrowers play the **"No Manual Review" Game,** which is structuring their credit profiles so the application glides straight through the system with no red flags, no pauses, no questions.

WHY MANUAL REVIEW IS DANGEROUS

Think of automated approval like the express lane at the airport. If you clear TSA PreCheck, you walk right through. Manual review is the other line, the one where they take off your shoes, pull out your bags, and start asking questions you weren't ready for.

The dangers include:

- **Lower Limits** – Humans tend to approve for less than algorithms.
- **More Documentation** – You'll be asked for tax returns, bank statements, or proof of income.
- **Higher Decline Rates** – If anything doesn't match up, the human underwriter can hit deny on the spot.

WHAT TRIGGERS MANUAL REVIEW

Applications get flagged for review when the system sees something out of line. The most common triggers are:

1. **High Utilization** – Carrying balances close to your limits.
2. **Too Many Recent Inquiries** – Multiple apps spread out over weeks, instead of one cycle.
3. **Derogatories** – Recent lates, collections, or charge-offs.
4. **Instability** – Multiple address changes, new jobs, or mismatched data on your application.
5. **Income Red Flags** – Reporting income that doesn't align with your credit history or banking activity.

HOW TO AVOID MANUAL REVIEW

Here's how to structure your profile so your applications stay in the fast lane:

1. **Run Funding Cycles, Not Random Apps**
   - Apply for everything in one sweep. Don't spread it out. Inquiries not yet reporting give you a window of

opportunity to stack approvals before the system catches up.

2. **Keep Utilization Low**
   - Under 10% utilization tells the algorithm you're not desperate for credit. Over 50% almost guarantees manual review.

3. **Season Accounts Before Funding**
   - Let new accounts "age" 90–120 days before another cycle. Too many fresh accounts are a red flag.

4. **Match Your Story**
   - Make sure your application lines up with your report. Job titles, addresses, and income should look consistent. Discrepancies scream fraud.

5. **Build Banking Relationships First**
   - Apply where you bank first. A strong interbanking credit relationship can override borderline data.

Case Study: Auto Approval vs. Manual Review

Erica had a 695 score but ran her funding cycle right. Utilization was at 7%, her last late payment was three and a half years ago, and she applied for seven cards in the same week. Five out of seven were approved automatically, $61,000 in total funding... because nothing triggered manual review.

Sean, on the other hand, had a 748 credit score but carried 55% utilization and applied for one card in January, another in February, and another in March. By April, 14 hard inquiries had piled up; those other accounts looked too new, and the system flagged him. He got dragged into manual review and was denied for "excessive recent activity."

Same difference as always: structure beats score.

THE KEY TAKEAWAY

The "No Manual Review" Game is simple: build your profile to slide through the automated systems. Keep utilization low, time your cycles, stay consistent, and never give the system a reason to stop your application for a second look. Also, try your best to keep all of the information the same as you have previously used, especially because addresses, phone numbers, and occupations get reported to your credit report. Remember, that's another one of The Great American Credit Secrets.

Because once you're in manual review, you're negotiating. But if you avoid it altogether, you're already approved before anyone has time to blink.

THE PSYCHOLOGY OF MANUAL REVIEW

To understand how to avoid it, you've got to know how underwriters think once your application lands on their desk. Automated systems are cold and logical... just math. Humans, on the other hand, bring **bias, caution, and personal judgment.**

Here's what happens when you're flagged for review:

- The underwriter looks for reasons to **justify the algorithm's hesitation.**
- They scan for inconsistencies: "Does this story add up?"
- They compare your profile against the bank's policies line by line.
- If anything feels off, their instinct leans toward protecting the bank, not approving you.

That's why avoiding manual review is so powerful: you remove human hesitation from the process.

EXTRA TRIGGERS THAT GET OVERLOOKED

We covered the main triggers already, but here are a few more people don't realize can get them flagged:

- **Income Mismatch**: If you claim $150,000 in annual income but your credit history doesn't show accounts consistent with that level, you'll raise eyebrows. Claiming that you make $400,000-$600,000 or more will normally **always** get flagged. Even if it's true. If you earn that much, it's better to sit down with a banker and apply for the funding you need.
- **Fraud Databases**: Banks use shared databases like ChexSystems and Early Warning Services. If you've bounced checks or had accounts closed, those records can quietly push you into review.
- **Thin Files with High Scores**: Believe it or not, a 750 score with only two accounts looks suspicious. The system asks, "How did this person build such a high score with so little history?" It also looks as if you do not have a lot of history dealing with multiple lenders... another red flag.
- **Too Many New Accounts**: Opening more than three or four new tradelines in under six months often signals risk. That's why whenever you open accounts, ideally you want them to sit for a minimum of six months before you start applying again.

*Remember: banks use sophisticated algorithms to protect themselves and calculate who is the lowest risk for approval. Instead of trying to outsmart them, just know how to play the game, know exactly what they're looking for, and line up your profile to match what is attractive to them.

ADVANCED STRATEGIES TO STAY OUT OF REVIEW

1. **Strategic Staging**
   - Build your profile **90–120 days before** funding. Pay down balances, add tradelines, and let them season. By the time you apply, your file looks clean and aged.
2. **Data Consistency Audit**
   - Before applying, pull all three reports. Check addresses, job titles, phone numbers, even middle initials. If your identity looks messy, the system throws a flag. Clean it up before you apply.
3. **Income Realism**
   - Don't inflate income numbers to "look good." Lenders compare income to credit behavior. If you say you earn $200,000 but have a $2,000 limit card as your highest, you look inconsistent. Always match your income to your credit history. Note: If you work at Starbucks as a team lead but put $100,000 on the application, it will normally get flagged. This does not add up.
4. **Know Your Bank's Appetite**
   - Every lender has its sweet spot. Some love business funding. Some prefer mortgages. Some tighten on high-risk industries. Research before applying so you

don't waste inquiries on a bank that wasn't going to approve you anyway.

5. **Pre-Qualification Tools**
   - Many banks now offer "soft pull" pre-approvals. Use them. If you're pre-qualified with solid terms, you're less likely to hit manual review once you move forward.

REAL-WORLD EXAMPLES IN PLAY

- **Business Owner Example**: Carla had a 715 score and low utilization. She ran all her applications in one week and kept her income claims modest and consistent. End result: $80,000 across three banks, all auto-approved.
- **Messy File Example**: Jason had a 765 score but three different addresses on his reports, a P.O. box listed, and inconsistent job titles. The algorithm flagged him. Manual review pulled his application apart. He ended up with a single $5,000 approval instead of the $40,000 he expected.

WHY THIS GAME IS EVERYTHING

If you master the "No Manual Review" game, you flip the odds dramatically in your favor. Instead of playing defense with under-writers, you glide through approvals like clockwork.

It's the difference between:

- Walking into a bank, hoping someone "likes" your file.
- Versus structuring your file so the system approves you before anyone has time to second-guess.

And once you've done this a few times, you'll see just how powerful it is to never even touch the manual review pile.

AFTER THE KEY TAKEAWAY: TRIGGERS IN THE 2025 LENDING WORLD

In 2025, banks aren't just checking your credit report. They're running your application through layers of technology that are smarter, faster, and harder to beat than anything we saw a decade ago. That's why understanding insider triggers is more important now than ever.

AI-Powered Fraud Detection

Most major banks and fintechs now use artificial intelligence to scan applications for subtle fraud patterns. Here's what that looks like:

- **Device/IP Tracking** – If you apply for multiple accounts in one day from the same device or through a VPN, the system could flag it.
- **Geo-Mismatch** – Applying from California with a home address in New York can look like fraud, even if you're traveling. This is because they track your IP Address. Best practice is to apply at home.
- **Behavioral Analytics** – AI watches how fast you type your Social Security number, how long it takes to complete a form, and whether you hesitate on income fields. Unusual behavior gets flagged.

The Velocity Trap

Velocity is how fast you're moving with applications. Banks share data across networks. If you submit five apps in a morning and three more that afternoon, the system can instantly mark you as a "credit seeker." That label doesn't just kill one application; it can shut down an entire funding run. This is rare, but something to look out for.

Income & Occupation Cross-Checks

Here's a 2025 reality: banks are cross-referencing income claims against occupational averages in real time.

- A "manager" claiming $150,000? Possible.
- A "cashier" claiming $150,000? Instant red flag.
- Even "entrepreneur" is now scrutinized: algorithms scan your deposits and business registrations to see if your story holds up. And it's vague, so I would caution against this; it falls in the "self-employed" category.

AI FRAUD DETECTION IS WATCHING EVERYTHING NOW

Banks and fintechs are using the most advanced fraud systems in history. These systems run in the background while you apply and quietly decide whether you look like a trusted customer or a potential threat. Here's how it really works according to insider data and real industry tools.

A. DEVICE AND IP TRACKING

Major institutions scan your digital footprint instantly.

Chase, Capital One, Citibank, American Express, Discover, plus fintechs like **Mercury, Brex, SoFi, Chime, and Revolut**, all use AI models that watch for:

- The device you are using
- Your IP address
- Your browser fingerprint
- VPN or proxy activity
- Multiple applications from one device in a 24-hour window

Capital One, Synchrony, and Brex Financial are especially aggressive. If the same device pushes too many applications too fast, your risk score spikes, and the system treats you like a potential fraudster.

Geo mismatches also count. Applying from California with a New York residential address tells banks like Citi and Wells Fargo that something does not line up, and it weakens your trust profile.

B. BEHAVIORAL BIOMETRICS

This is the hidden technology most people never think about.

Banks use behavioral data partners like **ThreatMetrix, BioCatch, TransUnion FraudGuard, and Experian CrossCore** to analyze small details such as:

- How fast you type your Social
- Whether you type it or paste it
- How long you pause on income fields
- Mouse movement patterns
- Touchscreen pressure on mobile
- Typing rhythm, cadence, and hesitation

If your behavior resembles stolen identity patterns or scripted applications, banks such as Chase and AmEx immediately route you to deeper risk scoring.

C. THE RELATIONSHIP OVERRIDE ADVANTAGE

Even with all this AI watching everything, one thing still beats the machines.

Relationship credit, also known as interbanking credit, can override low-level flags that would defeat a brand-new applicant. Banks reward loyalty because they trust the financial patterns they see over time.

Here is how different institutions treat their existing clients:

A. CHASE

Loyalty is everything. Long-term checking or business banking relationships often push borderline applications into approval instead of auto-denial.

B. WELLS FARGO

Internal customers get escalated to manual review instead of being killed by automated fraud filters.

C. CREDIT UNIONS

Places like **Navy Federal, Patelco, Golden 1, SDCCU, and Teachers FCU** operate with a member-first culture. If you have history with them, they may greenlight approvals that big bank algorithms would shut down immediately.

REAL-WORLD EXAMPLE

Imagine two people applying for the same card at the same moment.

Jessie applies from a hotel in Miami using a VPN. He submits four applications back-to-back using the same phone. He pastes his social, hesitates on income, and types too fast on the final page. The AI system sees: new device, mismatched geo data, copy-and-paste social, rapid-fire submissions, and highly bot-like behavior. His application gets flagged instantly and routed to auto-decline.

Shelah applies from home using the same computer she has used to log into her Chase checking account for five years. She has steady deposits hitting every month. Even though her geo data looks slightly unusual and the system catches a pause on the income field, Chase sees ten thousand data points of stable history. The relationship override takes control, and Shelah gets approved on the spot.

REAL-WORLD ILLUSTRATION: 2025 APPROVALS AND DENIALS

- **Fintech Example**: A client with a 710 score was instantly denied for a personal loan because the AI system flagged that he applied from a hotel Wi-Fi network in another state. To the algorithm, it looked like identity fraud.

- **Credit Union Example**: Another client with a 660 score got approved for a $5,000 loan because she'd been with the same credit union for twelve years and had consistent direct deposits. Her interbanking credit overrode her weak public score.
- **Big Bank Example**: An applicant with a 780 score was denied for a $25,000 card because his file showed four new accounts in the past 90 days. The system didn't care about his "excellent" score; it cared about his velocity.

FINAL WORD ON TRIGGERS

In today's lending environment, it's not enough to just build a strong profile; you have to play defense against the triggers. One wrong move can flip your file from "approved" to "denied" in seconds.

The good news is that once you understand these hidden signals, you can prepare ahead of time. Remove the red flags, highlight the green, and let the system say yes before a human ever gets involved.

BEYOND THE ALGORITHM: THE BUSINESS OF LENDING

Here's the part most people miss: banks don't just approve or decline based on risk—they're also driven by **profitability.** Every "yes" or "no" is a business decision, not just a credit decision.

Think about it: banks don't make money by saying no all the time. They make money by lending to people who look like they'll pay them back, with interest. That's why some "risky" clients still get approved, while others with higher scores get turned down.

PROFIT TRIGGERS BANKS SAY "YES" TO

- **Revolving Revenue Potential**: Clients who carry a small balance and pay interest are highly profitable. Too much balance = risk. Zero balance = no revenue. The sweet spot is the borrower who pays most months but occasionally carries a little.
- **Cross-Sell Opportunities**: If your profile shows potential for multiple products—credit card, auto loan, mortgage—the bank sees long-term value. Approvals come easier when they think you'll deepen the relationship.
- **Deposit Activity**: Healthy checking and savings deposits signal that you'll use the bank for more than just credit. That makes you worth more to them.
- **Business Potential**: If your personal file looks solid *and* you own a business, banks see an opening for future lending. They may approve today's application as a way to set up tomorrow's deal.

WHEN BANKS SAY "NO" EVEN IF YOU LOOK GOOD

- **Unprofitable Profiles**: Believe it or not, some people look *too safe*. If you always pay in full, never carry balances, and barely use credit, you may get smaller limits. Why? Because you're not profitable. In other words, they'd rather lend money to someone who's gonna use it so that they can get paid interest from it.

- **Industry Bias**: Certain job titles or industries (gig work, cannabis, crypto) are treated as unstable. Even if your credit is strong, the bank's internal policy might mark you high-risk.
- **Portfolio Balance**: Banks don't want too much exposure in certain credit categories. For example, if they've already issued a lot of high-limit cards in a quarter, they may tighten up temporarily (even on good profiles).

Case Study: When Business Incentives Override Risk

Angela had a 690 score and moderate utilization. Normally, she'd be on the bubble for a high-limit card. But she had $20,000 sitting in a checking account at the same bank, plus steady direct deposits from her employer. The bank saw her as valuable beyond the credit card, so she was approved for $15,000.

Mark had a 770 score, low utilization, and zero derogatories. But he was the type of customer who always paid in full and barely used credit. To the bank, he looked unprofitable. He applied for the same card as Angela and was approved for only $5,000.

THE PSYCHOLOGY OF THE UNDERWRITER

When a human underwriter gets involved, psychology plays a bigger role than most people realize. They're not just evaluating your file—they're evaluating your story.

- **Consistency Calms Them**: Same address, same job, same income bracket = safety.
- **Confusion Concerns Them**: If your file raises questions

(Why so many new accounts? Why inflated income?), they lean toward "no."

- **Confidence Closes Them**: Applications that make sense, line up with the data, and tell a believable story slide through.

Remember: underwriters aren't rooting for you to win—they're rooting for themselves not to lose. The clearer and safer your story looks, the more likely they are to sign off.

THE KEY EXPANSION

So yes, the algorithms run the show in 2025. They scan, measure, judge, and decide in silence. But behind every "yes" or "no" is something deeper, something most people never think about. There is the business model of the bank and the human psychology of the underwriter watching from behind the glass.

If you want to beat the game, you cannot rely on a strong credit profile alone. You have to build a story that the system wants to invest in. A story that feels profitable, steady, and impossible to ignore.

Because inside the vault, credit is not just data.

It is narrative.

It is perception.

It is the quiet psychology of approval.

Master that, and the next chapter opens a door most people never even find.

SEVEN

THE PSYCHOLOGY OF HIGH-LIMIT APPROVALS

HOW BANKS DECIDE WHO GETS $20,000 AND WHO GETS $2,000

Before we go any further, you should know one thing: the real decisions are never made on paper. They are made in the shadows, where banks judge you long before you realize you are being watched.

If you've made it this far in the book, you already know the surface-level version of why banks approve or decline. But now we are stepping into something deeper. Something most borrowers never think about. Something most bankers could never explain, even if you sat them down and begged for clarity.

This chapter is not about the mechanics of credit.

This chapter is about the **mindset of lenders**.

It is about the quiet psychological signals that separate a $2,000 credit card approval from a $20,000 approval, or a $5,000 personal loan from a $50,000 personal loan.

Because here is the truth.

Banks are not just analyzing your credit profile.

As we mentioned before, they are analyzing **you**.

Your behavior.

Your patterns.

Your predictability.

Your psychology as a borrower.

And once you understand what lenders are actually "reading" in your profile, you can engineer the kind of applicant banks fight to give money to.

Welcome to the inner circle. Let's get into it.

THE FIRST SECRET: HIGH-LIMIT APPROVALS ARE EMOTIONAL DECISIONS DRESSED UP AS DATA

People love to believe banks are purely logical. They imagine a credit analyst staring at screens of numbers, crunching formulas, eliminating emotion. But the truth is different.

Underwriting is math.

High-limit approvals are psychology.

Banks want to feel confident about one thing above all else:

Will this person behave predictably with a large amount of credit?

Predictability is safety.

Safety is trust.

Trust is high limits.

If your profile radiates stability, discipline, and consistency, the bank's internal models confidently say yes to larger limits. If your file sends mixed signals, the algorithms pull back. Humans pull back. Everything tightens.

High-limit approvals are always given to the borrower who looks like they will not panic, not overspend, and not default. It is as simple and as powerful as that.

THE THREE TRAITS THAT SIGNAL "BIG LIMIT ENERGY"

Every high-limit borrower has the same three traits. These are psychological markers, not credit scores. Banks read these from your behavior, not your numbers.

Let's break them down.

1. STABILITY: THE FOUNDATION OF HIGH LIMITS

Nothing matters more.

If you look stable, you look fundable.

Banks evaluate stability by scanning for patterns like:

- Time at current residence
- Time at current employer
- History of steady income
- Predictable banking patterns
- Consistent addresses on file
- Identical information across all bureaus

A person who stays at an address for years looks different than someone moving every eight months. A person with a three-year job history looks different than someone jumping industries every season.

Stability says one thing to a bank:

You are predictable.

Predictable borrowers get higher limits.

2. CONTROLLED UTILIZATION: THE DISCIPLINE FACTOR

Every high-limit borrower shows restraint on their credit cards. Banks read low utilization not just as strategy, but as psychology.

Low utilization says:

"I am in control."

"I use credit, but I do not depend on it."

"I am responsible with my access to capital."

High utilization says:

"I am overwhelmed."

"I am stressed."

"I am dependent on credit for survival."

High-limit approvals go to the borrowers who look like they treat credit like a tool instead of a lifeline.

If your profile says "discipline," your limits explode.

3. MATURITY: DEPTH OF EXPERIENCE

Banks want to see that you have a history of managing credit successfully. They want to know you have been "trained" by the system.

Maturity looks like:

- Older accounts
- Larger limits already reporting
- Consistent on-time payments
- A good mix of accounts
- Low-risk behavior over years

Immature profiles attract low limits.

Mature profiles attract premium limits.

This is why accounts over three years old carry so much weight. It shows you have seen ups and downs and handled them responsibly. It shows you understand how credit works. You are not a rookie.

Banks love experience.

High limits go to experienced borrowers.

THE PRESTIGE MODEL: HOW YOUR OCCUPATION SHAPES YOUR LIMITS

This is one of the most misunderstood aspects of lending.

Your occupation changes how much banks trust you.

Not because they judge your job.

Because they judge your **stability**, **risk**, and **income predictability** based on your industry.

Certain roles naturally score higher on bank psychology:

- Nurses
- Engineers
- Government workers
- Teachers
- Military
- Long-term corporate employees
- Managers
- Supervisors
- Analysts
- Technicians

These occupations are considered stable, reliable, and structured. They attract higher limits.

On the flip side, occupations like:

- Construction labor
- Retail cashiers
- Gig workers
- Seasonal workers
- Recent self-employed
- Vague job titles like "entrepreneur"

… are viewed as unpredictable or volatile.

Banks are not judging a person's worth.

Banks are judging the **risk profile** of an occupation.

High-limit approvals follow these psychological assumptions.

THE PREDICTABILITY MATRIX: WHAT BANKS WANT TO SEE BEFORE GIVING YOU REAL MONEY

Here is the mental checklist banks run before approving a big limit. They want to know:

1. Do you look stable?
2. Do you look consistent?
3. Do you look responsible?
4. Do you look predictable?
5. Do you look profitable?

If you hit these five criteria, you will almost always land higher limits, even with a lower score.

This is why someone with a 690 gets a $20,000 card while someone with a 780 gets $2,000. It is not the number. It is the narrative.

High-limit approvals are narrative-based, not score-based.

THE SUBTLE BEHAVIORS THAT SIGNAL "SAFE BORROWER"

Banks look for behavior traits, not just data. Here are the psychological cues they reward:

- You rarely max out your cards
- You use credit regularly but not excessively
- You have minimal recent inquiries
- You do not open too many accounts too fast

- You pay early, not just on time
- You maintain consistent balances
- You avoid erratic swings in usage

These behaviors communicate one thing:

You think before you spend.

High-limit borrowers look strategic.

Low-limit borrowers look impulsive.

THE BORROWER ARCHETYPES BANKS LOVE (AND THE ONES THEY AVOID)

Based on millions of approvals, lenders have created profiles of borrowers they trust and borrowers they avoid.

Here are the three archetypes banks love:

1. THE PLANNER

Uses credit intentionally, low utilization, consistent payments, stable life.

This borrower gets premium limits.

2. THE PROFESSIONAL

Has a structured occupation or long-term employment history.

Banks see reliability and reward it heavily.

3. THE BALANCED BORROWER

Uses credit monthly, pays it down monthly, never pushes limits.

Banks see low volatility and high discipline.

Now for the three archetypes banks avoid:

A. THE SPRINTER

Opens many accounts fast, submits random applications, impulsive behavior.

High-risk psychology.

B. THE OVEREXTENDER

High utilization, high balances, low cash flow.

Appears stressed and unstable.

C. THE GHOST

Thin file, little experience, no depth.

Too unpredictable for large limits.

WHY BANKS REWARD PREDICTABILITY ABOVE ALL ELSE

If you take nothing else from this chapter, take this.

High-limit approvals have nothing to do with being "rich."

They have everything to do with being predictable.

Predictability lowers risk.

Lower risk means higher confidence.

Higher confidence means larger approvals.

People with stable, predictable profiles get bigger limits because banks know exactly what to expect from them.

People with erratic, unstable profiles get smaller limits because banks have no idea how they will behave.

Everything in this chapter comes back to the same idea.

High limits go to borrowers who look reliable.

Real-World Example: The 680 That Beat the 770

Meet Patty and Randy.

Randy has a 770 score. He is proud of it.

But he jumps jobs every year, has four recent inquiries, has two new cards, and carries 48% utilization.

He applies for a Chase Sapphire card and is approved for a $3,200 limit.

Patty has a 680 score.

But she has seven years at her job, four years at her address, low utilization, and deposits hitting her account every two weeks.

She applies for the same card.

She gets $18,300.

This is the psychology of lending.

It is not the score.

It is the stability.

It is the predictability.

It is the story.

THE KEY TAKEAWAY

High-limit approvals are not about credit scores.

They are about human behavior.

They are about how trustworthy you look to a bank before you ever speak a word. When your profile tells the story of a disciplined, stable, predictable borrower, your limits rise. When your profile looks scattered, impulsive, or inconsistent, your limits shrink.

Your public score is the headline.

Your borrower psychology is the entire story.

Once you understand this, you stop chasing numbers and start building yourself into the kind of borrower banks fight to approve.

EIGHT
THE RELATIONSHIP
CREDIT LOOPHOLE

HOW INSIDER CONNECTIONS, BANKING HISTORY, AND SOFT DATA BOOST YOUR LIMITS

The truth is simple and brutal: relationships can override the algorithm, but only if the banker believes you're worth the risk.

Here's one of the biggest secrets in lending: **relationships beat algorithms.** You can have an average credit score and still get funding that someone with a perfect profile can't touch, all because you've built trust with your bank.

This is what I call the **Relationship Credit Loophole.** It's the invisible side of credit approval, the part based not on numbers alone, but on how well the bank knows you, your history, and your overall value as a customer. So smile at your banker and call them by name when you walk inside the establishment... remember, you're playing to win.

WHY RELATIONSHIPS MATTER

Banks are businesses, and businesses invest in people they trust. A client they've seen for years that has consistently been depositing paychecks, paying off loans, keeping accounts active, will almost always get a longer leash than a stranger walking in the door with nothing but a high score.

Soft data: the non-score information banks consider, is where the loophole lives. Examples include:

- How long you've had accounts with them.
- How often you deposit funds.
- Whether you've paid off previous loans with them.
- Even how you interact with bank staff (yes, that matters).

HOW TO BUILD RELATIONSHIP CREDIT

1. **Start with Deposits**
   - Open checking and savings accounts with the bank or credit union you want to fund you.
   - Set up direct deposit so they see consistent money flowing in.
2. **Show Usage, Not Just Storage**
   - Banks like to see accounts in motion. Pay bills through them. Run transactions. Don't just park money.
3. **Season Your History**
   - Six months to a year of steady activity is often enough to build a foundation.
   - At the two-year mark, your relationship credit becomes very strong.
4. **Ask for the Right Products**
   - Once you've built history, ask for credit products that match your relationship. Business credit lines,

personal loans, or higher-limit cards often open up
easily.

5. **Leverage Human Connections**
   - Small banks and credit unions often rely on branch
     managers and loan officers. A good relationship with
     them can override an algorithm and fast-track
     approvals. They can even put in a call for a manual
     review or give you some insider tips. These extra
     perks can make all the difference.

Case Study: Relationship Credit in Action

Daniel's Direct Deposits

Daniel had a 685 score, not spectacular. But he'd been with his
credit union for nine years. His paycheck hit the same account
every two weeks, and he'd previously paid off a $12,000 auto loan
with them. When he applied for a $10,000 personal line of credit,
he was instantly approved, but without a manual review, no
hesitation.

Sophia's Shiny Score

Sophia had a 765 score but had just opened an account with the
same credit union three months earlier. No deposits, no history.
On paper, she looked stronger than Daniel. But she was denied for
the same $10,000 line. Why? Because she was an unknown.

INSIDER MOVE: RELATIONSHIP + TIMING

The loophole gets even stronger when you combine it with
timing. For example, banks often loosen approvals at the end of

quarters when they need to hit lending goals. If you're already a trusted member, you'll see your approvals come faster and bigger when the bank is hungry to move money.

WHY THIS LOOPHOLE WORKS IN 2025

With AI and automation running approvals, the human touch seems smaller. But relationship credit is still one of the few things that can override strict algorithms. Banks know algorithms miss context. Your **years of consistent deposits, loyal account activity, and repayment history** tell a story the algorithm can't always capture.

That's why relationship credit is the ultimate loophole; it takes you from being a number in the system to being a client the bank wants to invest in.

KEY TAKEAWAY

Credit isn't just about scores: it's about trust. Build trust with your bank, and you'll unlock approvals that outsiders never even get the chance to see.

DEEP DIVE INTO PERSONAL RELATIONSHIP CREDIT

When it comes to personal funding, banks want to know two things: *Can you pay?* and *Will you pay?*

Your credit score only answers half that question. Relationship credit fills in the rest.

- **The Human Side of Relationship Credit, Branch-Level Overrides**: At smaller banks and credit unions, branch managers and loan officers can push approvals through even when the system hesitates. A face-to-face conversation can literally unlock thousands of dollars. When a bank employee sees your confidence, hears your reasoning, and understands your goals, they are more likely to override automated flags because they are attaching your application to a real person and not just a score.

- **Direct Deposit Power**: A steady paycheck hitting your account tells the bank you have predictable income. Even if your score is shaky, regular deposits build confidence. Banks do not just look at your credit; they look at your behavior. When they see consistency, discipline, and loyalty through your deposit history, they start treating you like a long-term customer instead of a risk.

- **Paying Off Old Loans**: If you have borrowed from the bank before and paid them back, they see you as a proven asset. That history gives you leverage to negotiate for bigger lines next time. Anytime you have shown them you borrow responsibly, they shift you mentally from potential liability to trusted borrower, which can lead to faster approvals, higher limits, and fewer questions asked during the application process.

- **The Trust Effect**: Banks are still run by people, and people naturally trust what feels familiar. When you maintain relationships inside a branch, greet the staff, ask questions, or simply show up with professionalism, your name becomes recognizable. That familiarity softens the strictness of underwriting because you are now seen as a stable presence rather than an anonymous applicant. Human trust often fills the gap where algorithms fall short, and that trust can translate directly into higher approvals and stronger credit opportunities.

Real-World Illustration:

Case: Chris the Teacher

Chris had a 670 score... not terrible, not great. But he'd been with his local credit union for eleven years. His teacher's salary had been direct-deposited every two weeks since 2014. When he applied for a $20,000 line of credit, the system flagged him for manual review. The loan officer overrode it instantly: *"He's been with us for a decade. Approve it."* Chris walked out with the loan in 24 hours.

Lesson: Loyalty talks louder than a credit score.

BUILDING YOUR OWN RELATIONSHIP CREDIT STEP-BY-STEP

Choose Your Bank Wisely

Credit unions and regional banks often value relationships more than big national chains because they rely heavily on member loyalty and personalized service.

Plant Your Flag

Open checking and savings accounts and make them your primary banking home so the institution can see your financial behavior clearly.

Show Movement

Run bills, deposits, and even small loans through them because usage creates history, and that history becomes your credibility.

Ask for Small Credit First

Start with a $500 to $1,000 credit builder or secured loan and pay it off on time. Consistent repayment builds trust and creates a record the bank can rely on.

Climb the Ladder

Every six to twelve months, ask for higher limits or new products so you can slowly expand your profile within the same bank.

In Short

Treat your bank like a partner and not just a place to store money. Your behavior over time signals stability, reliability, and long-term potential. Added deposits, responsible usage, and steady communication all work together to help you build real relationship credit, which eventually unlocks approvals that algorithms alone would never grant.

PAGE 2: THE BUSINESS SIDE OF RELATIONSHIP CREDIT

Now, let's take this loophole to the next level: business funding. This is where relationship credit can transform an average business owner into a six-figure funding magnet.

SOFT DATA BANKS LOOK AT FOR BUSINESS

- **Deposit Patterns** – Do you have consistent revenue hitting your business checking account?
- **Longevity** – Has the account been active for a year or more?
- **Owner's Track Record** – If you've managed personal accounts well with the same bank, they'll trust your business accounts.
- **Industry Risk** – Some industries (restaurants, trucking, real estate) carry higher risk, but a strong banking history can override it.

INSIDER STRATEGIES FOR BUSINESS RELATIONSHIP CREDIT

1. **Run All Business Revenue Through One Bank**. Banks want to see inflows. If your deposits are spread across multiple accounts, consolidate them. This is neater and more appealing than multiple accounts with deposits spread out.
2. **Open Business Savings Early**. Even if you only park $100 in it, it signals long-term intent.
3. **Leverage Your Personal Relationship**. If you've had personal accounts with the bank for years, use that to negotiate business funding. "I've been a customer here for eight years; I want to grow my business with you, too."
4. **Time Your Applications**. End of quarter and end of year are prime times when banks are chasing lending goals. That's when your relationship pulls extra weight.

Case Study: Relationship Credit for Business

Case: Maria, the Salon Owner

Maria ran a small hair salon and had only a 680 personal score. Her business had $7,000–$10,000 in monthly revenue, all deposited into her local credit union for the past eighteen months. When she applied for a business line of credit, the algorithm flagged her industry as "medium risk." Normally, she'd be denied or given a low limit.

But her banker overrode the system, saying: *"She's been steady with us for eighteen months. Her deposits are consistent. Approve her."* Maria walked away with a $25,000 business line of credit.

THE BIG PICTURE

Whether it's personal or business, relationship credit is the loophole that gives you leverage that algorithms can't calculate. It's not just about what's on paper; it's about trust, loyalty, and history.

When you master relationship credit, you stop competing with strangers. You create a back door that gets you approved even when the numbers aren't perfect.

Case Study: Two Paths, Two Outcomes

Let me give you a real-world example of how relationship credit flips the script.

Case 1: Jamal, the Newcomer

Jamal had a 750 personal credit score, no late payments, and utilization under 10%. On paper, he looked golden. But when he applied for a $15,000 personal loan at a national bank, the system ran him straight through automation. No history with the bank. No deposits. No prior loans. The algorithm spit out a $5,000 approval, and that was with documentation required.

Jamal walked away frustrated. *"How did I get such a low limit with a 750?"* The answer: he had no relationship with the bank. He was just a number in their system.

Case 2: Karen, the Insider

Now compare that with Karen. Her personal score was only a 695 which was not bad, but definitely weaker than Jamal's. But Karen had been with her regional credit union for nine years. Every paycheck hit her checking account like clockwork. She'd financed a car with them in the past and paid it off early. The staff knew her name.

When Karen applied for the same $15,000 personal loan, the system initially flagged her for a lower approval. But the loan officer reviewed her file and said, *"She's been with us forever. Approve the full $15,000."* No extra documentation, no delays. Just a stamp of approval.

THE LESSON

Jamal had the stronger score, but he was a stranger. Karen had the weaker score, but she was family. And in banking, family wins.

When a bank feels like you are one of their own, they will go to bat for you in ways that make you realize the real cheat code in finance is showing up consistently and letting your presence build the kind of quiet respect money alone can't buy.

THAT'S THE RELATIONSHIP CREDIT LOOPHOLE

It's proof that in today's system, numbers matter, but relationships can rewrite the outcome completely.

It reminds you that even in a world full of algorithms and rigid underwriting, being known, being trusted, and being steady still has the power to flip the whole board in your favor.

BREAKING DOWN THE RELATIONSHIP ADVANTAGE

The Jamal vs. Karen story isn't just a nice illustration; it's also a blueprint. Let's unpack why Karen won, even though her score was weaker.

If you pay attention to the hidden moves in her situation, you can literally reverse engineer a playbook that shifts you from outsider energy to VIP treatment without ever raising your voice or begging for approval.

1. TRUST OVER NUMBERS

Banks don't lend just to scores; they lend to people. Jamal's 750 score made him look great to the algorithm, but the bank had zero evidence of how he behaved with their money. Karen's 695 score wasn't as pretty, but her years of deposits, loan payments, and account activity told the bank everything it needed, which is that she could be trusted.

The truth is that trust leaves a trail, and when you build that trail inside one institution, it becomes a quiet superpower that lets you win even when the numbers say you should lose.

2. LOYALTY AS LEVERAGE

Karen wasn't just another applicant; she was their customer. Banks compete for loyalty. If you've shown commitment to them for years, they see you as an investment worth protecting. That's why her loan officer was willing to override the system. Jamal, meanwhile, was free to walk out the door and bank somewhere else.

Loyalty turns you from a name on an application into someone the bank feels obligated to take care of, and that kind of energy can move mountains when everyone else is stuck fighting the algorithm.

3. THE VISIBILITY FACTOR

Think about this: banks can't see what you're doing at other banks. Jamal may have a perfect history somewhere else, but his new bank only saw a blank slate. Karen had all her activities visible in-house. That visibility gave her an edge the algorithm couldn't calculate.

When a bank can literally watch your financial habits unfold inside their own system, you stop being a mystery and start being a sure thing, which is exactly the kind of confidence lenders love to reward.

4. THE HUMAN OVERRIDE

At the end of the day, Karen had something Jamal didn't have, which was a human advocate. When a banker knows you by name, when they've seen you for years, they'll vouch for you. And in cases like hers, that personal vote of confidence can unlock thousands of dollars instantly.

There is nothing more powerful in banking than having someone on the inside who genuinely believes in you because that single connection can open doors that algorithms, credit scores, and perfect applications will never open on their own.

APPLYING THIS LESSON TO YOUR OWN PROFILE

If you're reading this and thinking, *"Well, I don't have that kind of history with my bank,"* here's the good news: you can start building it today.

- **Choose one primary bank or credit union** and commit to it.
- **Run your life through that account**—paychecks, bills, small loans.
- **Get face time** with bankers and loan officers. Be more than a name on paper.
- **Stack history year by year** until you're the person they override the algorithm for.

Because in the credit game, relationships don't just soften the edges—they rewrite the rules.

PAGE 1: A HISTORICAL PERSPECTIVE

Before algorithms, lending was almost entirely about relationships.

Go back to the early 1900s, and if you wanted a loan, you did not have a credit score to show. You had your word, your reputation, and your history with the banker in your town. The banker knew who you were, knew your family, and maybe even saw your deposits come in every Friday from the local mill.

That trust was the original credit system. If you had a good relationship, you got funded. If you did not, you were out.

When FICO scores became the standard in the 1980s, banks started leaning less on personal trust and more on numbers. But here is the thing, relationship credit never disappeared. It simply became hidden inside soft data that still shapes decisions behind the scenes.

That is why in 2025, even with AI dominating, banks still reward long-term loyalty. History has proven one thing: people with consistent and visible banking relationships default less.

And if you really pay attention to how the world works, you will notice that the people who win are usually the ones who build real relationships, because the universe has a funny way of opening doors for people who show up consistently and let their character speak louder than their credit score.

PAGE 2: THE MODERN HYBRID

Today's system is a mix of cold data and warm relationships.

The Algorithm's Job: Scan files flag risks, approve or decline instantly.

The Relationship's Job: Provide context, trust, and history that can override the algorithm.

This is why relationships rewrite the rules. Algorithms can only see numbers. Relationships add a story.

Think about Karen from the earlier case study. On paper, she was weaker than Jamal. But her story, her nine years of loyalty, consistent deposits, and a paid-off loan, was worth more than his raw score.

That is why loan officers, branch managers, and even AI models trained on customer history give preference to people with deep relationships. They know loyalty equals lower risk.

HISTORICAL PROOF

Even during the 2008 financial crisis, borrowers who had long-standing relationships with local banks and credit unions were more likely to get emergency loans and extensions than strangers with higher scores. Trust beat numbers.

In 2020, during the COVID relief programs, businesses that had established banking relationships received PPP funds faster and in higher amounts than businesses that did not. Again, relationships rewrote the rules.

It all shows that no matter how advanced the financial world becomes, being known, being trusted, and being consistent still puts you in a different category, and that category gets privileges that algorithms could never justify on paper, but humans can feel instantly.

PAGE 3: WHAT THIS MEANS FOR YOU

Understanding this history should shift the way you approach funding. Do not just chase high scores, chase strong relationships.

Pick Your Main Bank

Stop bouncing between accounts. Choose a bank or credit union you want to grow with.

Run Consistent Activity

Banks trust what they see. Direct deposits, bill pay, and loan repayments create a digital history that algorithms cannot ignore.

Leverage History in Applications

When applying, highlight your tenure. For example, "I have been a customer here for seven years." That statement alone can shift a decision in your favor.

Use Relationship to Offset Weak Spots

If you have a 680 score but five years of deposits and no over-drafts, your bank may still approve you where another bank would decline.

Think Long-Term

The funding game is not about one approval. It is about positioning yourself so banks compete to give you money over the next ten years.

The Key Shift

When you understand that relationships rewrite the rules, you stop stressing over every little point on your credit score. Instead, you focus on building stability, loyalty, and visibility with the institutions you want to grow with.

And the moment you embrace that mindset, you move from hoping the system treats you fairly to mastering the game completely, because you are now operating with an advantage that cannot be copied, predicted, or beaten by anyone who only relies on their score.

TIMELINE: THE EVOLUTION OF RELATIONSHIP CREDIT

1900s – Trust & Reputation Era

- No credit scores.
- Loans based on local trust, word-of-mouth, and your banker knowing your family.
- Relationships are everything.

1950s – Early Credit Bureaus

- Credit reporting agencies begin tracking payment histories.
- Relationships still matter, but paper files start replacing memory and personal reputation.

1980s – FICO Takes Over

- FICO scores become the standard measure of risk.
- Algorithms gain power, but relationship credit lingers in the background through branch-level overrides and loyalty perks.

2008 – Financial Crisis

- Banks tighten credit across the board.
- Borrowers with strong relationships to local banks and credit unions often get loans extended, refinanced, or forgiven.
- Strangers to the bank? Declined.

2020 – Pandemic & PPP Loans

- Government launches Paycheck Protection Program.
- Businesses with banking relationships get funds quickly.
- Many without relationships couldn't even get their applications reviewed before money ran out.

2025 – AI in the Vault

- Artificial intelligence dominates underwriting.
- Algorithms scan velocity, utilization, job titles, and fraud indicators in seconds.
- But relationship credit is still the only factor that can override red flags—banks continue to trust loyal customers over strangers.

LESSON FROM HISTORY:

No matter how much technology changes the game, relationships remain the one constant that can rewrite the rules of credit.

And if you look closely at every era of banking, you will see the same hidden pattern where the people who build real connections glide through doors that stay locked for everyone else, almost like the system recognizes them before they even speak.

FINAL REFLECTION: TURNING RELATIONSHIPS INTO LEVERAGE

Here's the truth most people miss: your credit score is just the entry ticket, but your relationship is the VIP pass.

A score tells the bank you can handle credit. A relationship tells them you will. That difference is everything.

Think about it:

The stranger with an 800 score still gets declined if their profile looks unstable.

The loyal member with a 680 often walks out with a loan, a card, or a line of credit, sometimes faster, sometimes bigger.

That's not luck. That's the loophole.

And the moment you truly understand that the bank sees you not just as a number but as a pattern they trust, you start moving with the kind of confidence that turns even average profiles into unstoppable funding machines.

WHY THIS MATTERS FOR YOU

Most people treat banks like utilities. They open accounts, park money, and forget about them. That's a mistake. Banks reward activity, history, and loyalty.

Your checking account isn't just where your paycheck lands, it's proof of consistency.

Your savings account isn't just storage, it's proof of discipline.

Your past loans aren't just debts, they're receipts showing you can be trusted again.

When you start seeing every account, every deposit, and every interaction as part of your relationship credit score, you'll begin to understand why relationships rewrite the rules.

And once that clicks, you stop moving like a customer and start moving like someone who knows the secret handshake, because every little action you take inside that bank quietly builds the leverage you will use later when it matters most.

A CALL TO ACTION

If you're serious about unlocking the big funding, $50,000, $100,000, even $250,000—don't just chase scores. Chase trust.

Choose a bank or credit union and go all in.

Build history and let it season.

Treat your banker like a partner, not a gatekeeper.

Because when the day comes that you need six figures of funding, you won't be standing in line hoping an algorithm says yes. You'll already be on the inside track, with bankers and systems working in your favor.

And the beautiful part is that once you have earned that insider momentum, the approvals start to feel less like miracles and more like the natural result of a relationship you built with intention and strategy.

CLOSING THOUGHT

In the end, the Relationship Credit Loophole reveals a truth most borrowers never see until the consequences are staring them in the face: the system isn't neutral. It watches. It remembers. It studies the tiny details most people think don't matter.

The way you greet a teller.

The tone you use when asking a question.

The deposits you make when things are steady.

The restraint you show when things get tight.

Every action leaves a trail.

Every trail paints a story.

And that story decides who gets treated like a customer... and who gets treated like an asset.

People obsess over scores, limits, and inquiries.

But banks pay attention to something deeper—the psychology of your behavior.

They fund the profiles that feel predictable.

They lean toward the people who move like they're already trusted.

They open doors for the ones who understand the silent rules of the room.

Most borrowers never figure this out.

They chase approvals while ignoring the relationship that makes approvals effortless.

They try to game algorithms while neglecting the human eyes watching behind them.

But you're not "most borrowers" anymore.

You've studied the shadows.

You've seen how the story is shaped long before an application is submitted.

You understand that trust, once built correctly, becomes a multiplying force.

And here's the shift that changes everything:

Once a bank decides you're worth betting on, the entire system tilts quietly in your favor.

Limits rise without a fight.

Rates drop without you asking.

Loan officers start calling you first.

And funding that once felt out of reach becomes routine.

The same maze that others get lost in becomes a straight hallway for you.

That's the power hiding in plain sight.

That's the advantage only insiders ever gain.

And that's the moment where the relationship becomes more valuable than the credit score itself.

Because when you master both the human game and the financial game, the vault doesn't feel locked anymore.

It feels like it's waiting for you.

The system shifts.

Your story shifts.

Your future shifts.

And that shift... is the quiet beginning of something much bigger than a loan or a limit.

The Great American Credit Secret

NINE
AI IN THE VAULT
HOW ARTIFICIAL INTELLIGENCE IS CHANGING BANKING

There is a moment in the lending world where the lights go quiet, the system wakes up, and something unseen decides who gets in and who gets shut out before anyone even knows a decision was made.

Back in the day, your loan application sat on a desk until a banker picked it up. Today, it runs through an AI engine in seconds. The truth is, artificial intelligence is now the first underwriter on almost every loan, credit card, or line of credit you apply for.

And the deeper you peer into how these systems operate, the more you realize you are not applying to a bank anymore; you are stepping into a silent, unmarked vault where an unseen intelligence scans your life and decides your fate long before a human ever sees your name.

AI does not get tired. AI does not miss details. AI does not give you a chance because you look trustworthy. It looks at patterns, probabilities, and signals, then decides if you are greenlighted or declined.

And if you really pay attention, you begin to understand that the machine is not judging you personally; it is decoding you like raw data in a cold room, searching for the faintest sign of weakness or strength, almost like it is dissecting your financial DNA.

That means the game has changed. To win in today's system, you do not just need to know credit; you need to understand how AI thinks.

Because once you comprehend the rhythm inside the machine and learn to shape your profile into the patterns it quietly rewards, you start walking through the system like someone who has already read the ending and knows exactly how to move inside the shadows where the real decisions are made.

HOW BANKS ARE USING AI IN 2025

1. **Risk Prediction**
   - AI predicts whether you'll default before you even swipe the card.
   - It compares you against millions of borrower patterns to decide if you're safe or high-risk.
2. **Fraud Detection**
   - Every application is scanned for suspicious behavior: mismatched addresses, device changes, or "velocity" (too many apps in too little time).
   - AI flags it before a human ever sees it.
3. **Behavioral Analysis**
   - AI doesn't just look at your credit report; it looks at how you spend. Do you pay Netflix on time? Do you

overdraft? Do you spike spending after every payday? These patterns matter.

4. **Dynamic Limits**
   o Banks now use AI to adjust your limits in real time. Pay on time, use credit wisely, and your limit grows. Miss a payment or push your utilization too high, and your limit shrinks instantly.

5. **Alternative Data**
   o Rent payments, utility bills, even your cell phone bill are now being fed into AI systems. If you've got thin credit, this data can help or hurt depending on how consistent you've been.

Case Study: AI Says Yes, Human Says No

Case: Marcus

Marcus applied for a business credit card. His 695 score wasn't spectacular, but his deposit history was stable, his utilization was under 10%, and his rent had been reported consistently. The AI flagged him as "low risk" and auto-approved him for $15,000.

Case: Susan

Susan had a 740 score but had high utilization and three new accounts in the past ninety days. The AI flagged her as "credit seeker." Instead of an instant approval, her file went to manual review—where a human underwriter cut her limit down to $3,000.

Lesson? AI isn't impressed by raw scores. It's impressed by patterns.

HOW TO BEAT THE AI

If you want to win against the vault's new gatekeeper, here's how to position yourself:

1. **Keep Utilization Clean** – AI spots desperation fast. Stay under 10% if possible.
2. **Season Your Accounts** – AI rewards longevity. Don't stack too many new tradelines at once.
3. **Show Consistency** – Steady deposits, steady payments, steady addresses. The more boring your file looks, the better.
4. **Limit Velocity** – Don't shotgun applications across ten banks in a week. AI networks share data.
5. **Leverage Alternative Data** – If your rent or utility bills are reported, make sure they're spotless.

THE FUTURE OF AI IN BANKING

There is a silent shift happening in banking right now, a shift so subtle most people will not notice it until the system is already judging them long before they even apply.

In the next three to five years, expect AI to get even sharper. Banks will use real-time data from your phone, spending apps, and even subscriptions to decide your limits and approvals. The line between personal life and credit will blur.

And as that line fades, the system begins to watch you in ways that feel less like banking and more like surveillance, quietly measuring the rhythm of your life to decide if you are a risk or an asset before you ever say a word.

But here's the key: while AI is cold and logical, relationships still rewrite the rules. AI may flag you, but a banker who trusts you can override the system. The future belongs to people who master both sides, the algorithm and the relationship.

And the ones who learn to navigate both worlds will move through the financial system like ghosts, slipping through locked doors that everyone else finds sealed shut.

BUILDING ON PART 2: IN THE AGE OF AI

If you read *The Great American Credit Secret Part 2: In the Age of AI*, you already know that artificial intelligence has been reshaping the lending landscape. Back then, I showed you how AI was creeping into underwriting, fraud detection, and even funding decisions.

But what most people never understood was that AI was not creeping; it was preparing, quietly studying millions of profiles until it learned exactly how humans make mistakes and how to replace them.

But here in *Part 3*, we are no longer just in the age of AI; we are in the age of AI dominance. The banks are not experimenting anymore. They are not piloting new systems. They are running everything through AI by default.

What used to be a supporting role has now become the starring role.

And in this new era, the machine is not just helping the banker; the machine has become the banker, sitting silently in the center of the vault with the final word on your financial future.

THEN VS. NOW

Part 2 (Early AI)

AI was just starting to analyze credit data.

Banks still leaned on humans to double-check decisions.

Relationship credit was often the tiebreaker.

Part 3 (AI Dominance)

AI is the first and last line of approval.

Humans only get involved if the system flags something unusual.

Relationships are now the only factor that can override an algorithm's decision.

And somewhere in that shift, the power quietly transferred from people you could talk to into a system you can never see, a system that watches everything yet never explains why it chose the fate it handed you.

WHY THIS MATTERS TO YOU

The evolution matters because it explains why strategies from *Part 2* now look different in *Part 3*. Back then, you could still slip past AI if you had strong human relationships at the bank. Today, the system decides in seconds, and those relationships have shifted into a last line of defense.

That's why understanding insider triggers, fraud indicators, and relationship credit is more important than ever. You are not just playing against underwriters anymore; you are playing against machines.

And the truth is, machines have no sympathy, only patterns, which means the only path forward is to shape your life in a way that makes the pattern fall in your favor before the system even starts watching you.

THE BIG CONTINUITY

If *Part 2* was about waking up to the reality of AI, then *Part 3* is about mastering it. You cannot afford to ignore it, and you cannot outsmart it by chance. You need to know how the vault thinks and then design your profile to pass through it effortlessly.

That's what this chapter is all about. And by the time you are done, you will not only know how AI makes decisions, but you will know how to position yourself so it keeps saying yes to you while saying no to everyone else.

Because once you learn how to move inside the machine's logic, you start playing a different game entirely, a game where the system bends for you without ever realizing it has been outplayed.

THE SHIFT FROM ASSIST TO AUTHORITY

Back in *Part 2: In the Age of AI*, I told you AI was like the assistant in the room; it helped underwriters make decisions, but it did not run the show. Fast-forward to 2025, and now AI is the show.

Here's the evolution:

Yesterday, humans decided, and AI assisted.

Today, AI decides, and humans observe.

Tomorrow, AI decides, and humans barely get involved at all.

This matters because you can no longer rely on charm, explanations, or human flexibility. If the algorithm says no, you are already in the danger zone.

But here's the loophole: AI runs on patterns. If you understand the patterns it favors and the ones it hates, you can stack the odds in your favor before you even apply.

And once you understand those patterns, you begin moving like someone who can see the code running beneath the surface, adjusting your life in subtle ways that unlock approvals other people swear are impossible.

AI PATTERNS TO EMBRACE

- **Consistency**: Stable addresses, long-term employment, regular deposits.
- **Low Risk Ratios**: Utilization under 10%, steady payment history.
- **Seasoning**: Accounts that are aged and proven.
- **Moderation**: Not too many new accounts, not too many inquiries.

AI PATTERNS TO AVOID

- **Velocity**: Too many apps in too little time.
- **Mismatch**: Job title vs. income, address vs. location, profile vs. application.
- **Spike Behavior**: Maxing out cards, sudden changes in deposits, unusual spending.

AI isn't emotional—it's mathematical. But that's also why it's predictable if you know what to look for.

PAGE 2: PLAYING OFFENSE IN THE AI ERA

So how do you actually *use* this knowledge to your advantage? By going from passive borrower to **strategic player.**

STEP 1: PRE-CHECK YOURSELF LIKE AI WOULD

Before you apply, run a self-audit. Ask yourself:

- *Does my utilization look clean?*
- *Are my addresses and job info consistent across reports?*
- *Do I have too many new accounts in the last 90 days?*
- If the answer is shaky, fix it first. Don't walk into the vault unprepared.

STEP 2: BUILD AI-FRIENDLY DATA

AI feeds on patterns, so give it what it wants!

- Add trade lines that show consistency.
- Report rent or utilities if they're spotless.
- Keep deposits flowing steadily into one main account.

STEP 3: PROTECT YOUR PROFILE

AI systems are connected across banks. That means one mistake can echo everywhere.

- Don't shotgun apps across ten institutions.

- Don't overstate income because it will cross-check with averages.
- Don't play messy with addresses or mismatched data.

STEP 4: USE RELATIONSHIPS AS THE OVERRIDE

Even in 2025, relationships remain the "human override." If AI flags you, a banker who trusts you can still vouch for you. Build that safety net now before you need it.

FINAL WORD ON AI IN THE VAULT

There is a point in the process where the machine has already judged you, where the decision is made in a quiet instant long before you ever hear the result, and most people will never even realize that moment existed.

Artificial intelligence has flipped the game, but it has not killed your chances. In fact, if you know how it thinks, you have an edge most borrowers will never have.

And once you understand the hidden rhythm that drives these systems, you start to see the lending world not as a wall blocking you, but as a maze you can walk through with ease while everyone else gets lost in the dark.

Think of it this way: the average person is walking into the vault blind, hoping their score is good enough. But after reading this, you will be walking in with the cheat codes. You will know what patterns to build, what behaviors to avoid, and how to keep the system working in your favor.

And when you finally step into that digital vault with this level of insight, the silence no longer feels threatening; it feels familiar, almost like the system recognizes you as someone who belongs behind the curtain.

And that is how you win in the age of AI dominance.

Because victory does not come from luck, it comes from understanding the machinery inside the vault so well that the system starts saying yes to you automatically, while everyone else wonders why the rules suddenly stopped working for them.

And that's how you win in the game of influence.

TEN
THE BLACKLIST YOU DON'T KNOW YOU'RE ON

EARLY WARNING SYSTEMS, INTERNAL FRAUD DATABASES, AND CLEARING YOUR NAME

There is a hidden part of the financial system where your name can be marked long before you ever realize it, a place where silent flags and invisible files decide your fate without a single warning.

Here's a truth that rattles people every time I say it: your credit report isn't the only report banks look at.

And once you understand that the real judgment happens in files you never get to see, you realize how little control most people actually have over their own financial identity.

You can have a perfect 750 score, a spotless history, and a strong income, and still get denied instantly. Why? Because you're on a list you didn't even know existed.

And the scariest part is that these lists do not announce themselves; they do not notify you; they simply watch and block you in the shadows like a locked door you never knew was there.

Welcome to the world of early warning systems and internal fraud databases. These are the blacklists banks use to keep people out of the system. And if your name shows up on one of them, it doesn't matter what your credit score says; you're locked out until you clear it.

And once you truly grasp that a secret file can outrank your entire credit profile, you begin to see why knowing how to clear your name is not optional; it is survival inside the vault.

THE BIG BLACKLISTS

1. **ChexSystems**
   - Tracks your banking history, not your credit.
   - If you've ever overdrafted, bounced checks, or closed accounts with negative balances, it shows up here.
   - Too many marks? Banks deny you new accounts instantly.
2. **Early Warning Services (EWS)**
   - Owned by big banks like Chase, Wells Fargo, and Bank of America.
   - Flags suspected fraud, suspicious account activity, and even "velocity" if you open too many accounts too fast.
3. **Internal Bank Blacklists**
   - Each bank keeps its own private records.
   - If you burned them in the past, closed accounts in the red, unpaid charge-offs, they'll remember, even if your credit report looks clean.
4. **Fraud Prevention Networks**
   - Some institutions share data on suspected identity theft, account abuse, or loan defaults. Once flagged,

you can get shut down across multiple banks at once.

Case Study: The Invisible Denial

Case: Anthony

Anthony had a 745 score, low utilization, and stable income. On paper, he looked like the perfect applicant and should have been approved for a premium card without hesitation. But the decision came back instantly denied. Not because of his credit, not because of his income, but because of ChexSystems. Years earlier, he walked away from a checking account with a $90 overdraft that was never resolved. That $90 ghost followed him for years and slammed the door shut on funding he should have easily received. One forgotten mistake created a shadow that blocked his path until he paid it and cleared the record.

Case: Brianna

Brianna had a 680 score, lower than Anthony; nothing flashy on her profile, nothing extraordinary. But she had something Anthony did not. Her ChexSystems and Early Warning Services files were clean. No unresolved accounts. No suspicious closures. No hidden baggage. Her banking history showed consistency and discipline. When she applied for the same premium card, the approval was instant.

LESSON:

You can polish your credit score every day of the year, but if your name is sitting on one of these silent blacklists, you will never understand why banks keep shutting the door. These systems operate in the shadows, and until you shine a light on them, they can block you from approvals you should have earned.

HOW TO CHECK IF YOU'RE BLACKLISTED

1. **ChexSystems Report**
   - Go to ChexSystems.com and request your free annual report.
   - Dispute errors just like you would on a credit report.
2. **Early Warning Services Report**
   - Request a copy from earlywarning.com.
   - Look for flagged accounts, suspected fraud notes, or velocity alerts.
3. **Ask the Bank Directly**
   - If denied, ask, *"Was this decision based on ChexSystems, EWS, or internal records?"* They must tell you by law if a third-party system was used.

HOW TO CLEAR YOUR NAME

- **Pay Old Balances** – Even if it's years old, settle it. Banks respect cleared debts.
- **Dispute Errors** – Just like with credit bureaus, mistakes happen. File disputes with ChexSystems or EWS directly.
- **Wait It Out** – Most marks fall off after 5 years. If you can't clear it, sometimes time is your only option.
- **Leverage Relationships** – Some banks will overlook marks if you've built strong interbanking credit with them.

KEY TAKEAWAY

Credit isn't just about your FICO score; it's about your reputation in the entire financial system. Early warning systems and fraud databases are the secret walls that keep people out.

And the unsettling truth is that these walls are silent, invisible, and designed to judge you long before you ever realize you are being watched.

If you don't even know they exist, you'll keep running into invisible denials. But once you learn how to check them, clear them, and work around them, you take back control and unlock funding opportunities others can't even see.

Because the moment you uncover the hidden doors behind those walls, you stop moving like an outsider and start slipping through the system like someone who finally knows the layout of the vault.

WHERE THE BLACKLISTS CAME FROM

To understand why ChexSystems, Early Warning Services (EWS), and similar databases exist, you have to rewind to the 1970s and 80s. Back then, banks were getting hammered by fraud, overdrafts, and bad checks.

- **The Bad Check Epidemic:** Before debit cards, people used checks for everything. Bounced checks weren't just inconvenient—they cost banks millions every year.
- **Lack of Coordination:** One bank couldn't see if you had a negative account at another bank. That meant a customer could rack up overdrafts across multiple institutions with no one the wiser.

That's when banks realized they needed a **shared database**—a system to flag people with a history of bad banking behavior. Enter **ChexSystems**, founded in 1971. It became the central reporting agency for deposit accounts, similar to what Experian, Equifax, and TransUnion were for credit.

Fast-forward, and ChexSystems is now used by almost every major bank to decide whether to let someone open a checking or savings account.

THE RISE OF EARLY WARNING SERVICES

There is a part of the financial system that was built long before you ever opened your first account, a quiet network designed to watch everything and remember everything, even when you have forgotten it yourself.

By the late 1990s and early 2000s, banks were facing a new problem: fraud. Online banking was exploding, identity theft was on the rise, and criminals were exploiting gaps in the system.

And in the shadows of that chaos, the banks realized they needed something far more powerful than credit reporting, something that could see danger before it ever touched their vaults.

So, in 1995, the biggest banks in America, Wells Fargo, Bank of America, JPMorgan Chase, Capital One, and PNC, formed a joint company called Early Warning Services (EWS).

Unlike ChexSystems, which focused on overdrafts and unpaid accounts, EWS went deeper. It tracked:

Fraud attempts

Identity theft activity

Account velocity (how many accounts someone opened in a short time)

Suspicious transactions

EWS was designed to be a frontline fraud shield, and because it was owned by the biggest banks, it quickly became the standard across the industry.

And once it took root, EWS became a kind of financial surveillance grid, quietly connecting banks and allowing them to share warnings in real time about people the system decided were dangerous, whether they actually were or not.

WHY THIS MATTERS TO YOU

These companies weren't built to punish everyday people; they were built to protect banks from fraud and losses. But over time, the systems have gotten so strict that innocent mistakes can put you in the same category as fraudsters.

And that is the part most people never realize, that a moment of confusion or a single misunderstood transaction can place you in a digital file that shadows you for years.

Bounce a check in 2016? It's still on your ChexSystems report.

Open too many accounts too fast? EWS might flag you.

Dispute too aggressively? An internal blacklist could tag you.

The systems never forget, and that's what makes them so powerful.

Because once your name is inside one of those databases, you are no longer just a borrower; you are a risk profile, and the only way out is to learn how to navigate the same shadows where the system placed you.

PAGE 2: HOW THEY BECAME HIDDEN GATEKEEPERS

Once ChexSystems and EWS gained traction, other tools followed.

- **TeleCheck**: Used by retailers to screen checks at the point of sale.
- **Internal Blacklists**: Banks started keeping their own private lists of "problem customers." These aren't shared, but they're permanent. If you ever walked away owing a balance, they'll remember.

By the 2000s, almost every financial institution in America was tied into one or more of these systems. That means if you've ever been flagged, you're not just locked out of one bank—you're often locked out of the entire system.

THE POWER OF SHARED DATA

Here's the wild part: these databases are **not as heavily regulated as the credit bureaus.** While you have rights under the Fair Credit Reporting Act (FCRA) to dispute errors, the process is clunky, and banks have far more discretion.

That makes ChexSystems and EWS more like **gatekeepers** than scorekeepers. They don't care about your credit score, your income, or even your recent clean history. If you've got a mark, the door slams shut... period.

REAL-WORLD ILLUSTRATION

Think about it like this:

- **Credit Bureaus** decide how much credit you can get.
- **ChexSystems/EWS** decides if you can even step into the bank.

You can build a perfect 800 FICO, but if ChexSystems has you flagged, you might not even be able to open a basic checking account. That's how powerful these systems have become.

WHY YOU NEED TO CARE

There is nothing more dangerous in the financial system than an enemy you cannot see, and these databases can mark you long before you ever realize your name has been whispered in the shadows.

Most people never think about ChexSystems or EWS until they get blindsided by a denial. By then, it's too late; you're already flagged. That's why it's critical to:

Pull your reports proactively.

Clear old balances.

Build relationships with credit unions and community banks that may be more forgiving.

Because, whether you know it or not, these companies are shaping your financial future behind the scenes.

And once you understand that your fate can be decided quietly by systems you never signed up for, you begin to see why taking control early is the only way to stop the vault from closing its doors before you ever get to knock.

BEST PRACTICES TO STAY OFF THE BLACKLISTS

There is a quiet part of the system where names get marked, doors close without explanation, and a single forgotten detail can follow you like a shadow for years.

Getting flagged by ChexSystems, EWS, or an internal database can shut down your funding before it starts. The good news? You can avoid most of the traps with a few disciplined habits.

1. TREAT EVERY ACCOUNT LIKE IT'S PERMANENT

Never abandon a checking account, even if it's small. If you want to close it, make sure the balance is at zero, and all pending charges are clear. A $15 overdraft that sits too long can haunt you for years.

Because in the world behind the vault, even the tiniest unpaid amount can whisper to the system that you cannot be trusted, and once that whisper is recorded, it echoes longer than you think.

2. KEEP VELOCITY IN CHECK

Opening too many accounts in a short window is one of the fastest ways to trigger Early Warning Services. Spread your applications strategically, bundle credit pulls when you're in a funding cycle, then let your accounts season.

And understand this clearly: to the system, rapid movement looks like danger, and danger is a word that gets documented in places you will never see.

3. DON'T PLAY GAMES WITH MISMATCHED DATA

Banks and AI hate inconsistency. Make sure your name, address, and employer line up across your credit report, banking apps, and applications. Even small differences can look suspicious.

Because every inconsistency becomes a ripple in the system, and once enough ripples form, the machine assumes there is something beneath the surface you do not want it to find.

4. PAY SMALL BALANCES IMMEDIATELY

ChexSystems is not about big money; it is about patterns. Even a $25 unpaid overdraft is a red flag. Handle small balances before they become black marks.

In the vault, patterns speak louder than amounts, and a single careless oversight can stain your profile far more than a large debt paid responsibly.

5. BUILD RELATIONSHIPS WITH COMMUNITY BANKS AND CREDIT UNIONS

When the big banks say no, local institutions often say yes. They still check systems like EWS, but a strong relationship can some-times override the denial.

And if you ever find yourself locked out by the giants, it is the smaller institutions that can open doors you thought were sealed shut forever.

PAGE 4: THE MINDSET OF STAYING CLEAN

There is a way of thinking that keeps you invisible to the system's suspicion, and only the people who learn it stay untouched while everyone else walks straight into traps they never saw coming.

Here's what separates pros from rookies: mindset.

When you think like a banker, you don't just react; you anticipate. Your mindset should always be:

Consistency First: Keep your story simple, stable, and believable.

No Loose Ends: Close accounts cleanly, pay off small balances, and never leave errors unchallenged.

Assume You're Being Watched: Every application, every account, every deposit leaves a trail. Play as if it will be reviewed years later.

Think Long Game: Funding isn't about one approval; it's about building a reputation that keeps saying yes over and over.

And when you adopt this mindset, you move through the system like someone who understands the weight of every action, and the vault responds by treating you like someone who belongs on the inside.

SUB-BUREAUS: THE HIDDEN WATCHDOGS

There are layers beneath the layers, databases hidden under the mainstream ones, silently collecting pieces of your life and feeding them into the machine without ever asking your permission.

Most people know about Experian, Equifax, and TransUnion. But few realize there's an entire shadow layer of sub-bureaus tracking different parts of your financial life. By the way, if you hear someone saying, "Freeze these so that you can have better credit repair results," please ignore this. There are hundreds of hidden databases; this will only cause you grief, and you can still have successful results without freezing any of these.

LexisNexis

Tracks public records: bankruptcies, liens, judgments, even driving history.

Insurers, banks, and lenders use it to double-check your background.

Innovis

Known as the "fourth credit bureau."

Used heavily for identity verification, fraud checks, and specialty lending.

CoreLogic

Focuses on real estate, rental history, and evictions.

A bad rental report can block you from leases and certain loans.

TeleCheck

Monitors retail check-writing behavior.

Even if you don't use checks anymore, old flags can still show up.

These databases feed into the same decision-making systems that banks and AI rely on. That's why staying consistent across all parts of your financial life is crucial.

And the more you realize how these silent watchers share information, the more you understand that every part of your life leaves a trail that eventually finds its way back to the vault.

FINAL WORD ON MINDSET

Think of your financial footprint like a resume that never expires. Every account you open, every bill you pay, every record with your name on it—it's all being logged somewhere. The winners are the ones who respect that reality and move accordingly.

Because when you treat your financial identity like a weapon that must stay polished, you move differently, and the system responds by giving you access while quietly shutting the door on everyone else.

When you treat your credit, banking, and identity like assets that must stay polished, you stop playing defense and start playing offense. That's how you avoid the blacklist and build the kind of profile that gets approvals again and again.

And once you master this discipline, you stop fearing the vault and start navigating it with the calm certainty of someone who knows the rules better than the system itself.

ELEVEN
FUNDING STACKING
HOW THE PROS DO IT
WITHOUT GETTING FLAGGED

There is a moment in the funding world when the system stops guessing and starts watching, a moment when every move you make is recorded in silence, setting you up for either a flood of approvals or a quiet collapse you never see coming.

If you want six figures (or more) in available credit, you do two things well.

First, you build the right profile.

Second, you execute a funding cycle with military precision.

Funding stacking is not luck. It is a strategy. When done right, banks compete for your business. When done wrong, you trigger shutdowns, manual reviews, and low limits.

This chapter gives you the end-to-end system: what to prepare, the exact sequence to run, what to avoid, and how to recover if something goes off plan.

And once you understand how this system really works, the entire process starts feeling less like applying for credit and more like navigating a controlled operation inside the vault where every misstep has consequences.

THE HIGH-LEVEL PLAYBOOK

Prepare the file. Clean derogatories, align data, lower utilization, and season key tradelines.

Stage the bank list. Prioritize relationship banks, then predictable issuers, then opportunity lenders.

Execute the cycle in a tight window. Submit all target apps back-to-back in a planned order.

Manage post-approval flows. Let accounts report, pay down where needed, and use mirror effects to request increases.

Think of the funding cycle like a military sortie. Planning wins before combat begins.

Because in this game, precision is power, and the ones who move with discipline are the ones the system cannot deny.

WHO THIS WORKS FOR

Consumers seeking stacked personal credit.

Business owners combining personal and EIN-based business funding.

Anybody who wants predictable approvals rather than random wins.

This is not for people with unaddressed derogatories or open fraud flags. Do not stack until your file passes the basic checks.

And if you try to run this cycle with a dirty file, the system will catch you instantly, marking your name in places you never knew existed and shutting down your entire strategy before it even starts.

PRE-FLIGHT: 30 TO 0 DAYS BEFORE YOUR CYCLE

This is the preparation window. Do not rush it.

30 to 90 days out

- Pull all three credit reports and ChexSystems. Fix errors.
- Pay down revolving balances to under 10% ideally, under 30% minimum.
- Let any new tradelines sit at least 60 to 90 days for basic seasoning.
- Consolidate banking activity into one or two primary institutions to build interbanking credit.
- If you will use business funding, make sure business deposits are consistent for a minimum of three to six months.

7 to 30 days out

- Run a soft-pull prequalification at target issuers when available. Use pre-qual only if it does not create hard inquiries.
- Update and align application fields: job title, employer

name format, mailing address, phone. Make them match across reports.

- Identify which apps require full documentation and which are instant. Only include documents you can produce quickly.
- If you have any outstanding small overdrafts or ChexSystems items, settle them now. Even small balances can block openings.

0 to 3 days out

- Final utilization sweep. Pay down cards and keep balances low until after reporting.
- Make sure you are not traveling internationally when applying physically. Geo-mismatches trigger fraud filters.
- Put aside the documentation you may be asked for. Have PDFs ready: pay stubs, bank statements, EIN registration, business P&L if needed.

THE EXECUTION SEQUENCE: WHO TO HIT FIRST, SECOND, THIRD

Order matters. The sequencing below is what the pros use.

1. Relationship lenders first
   - Primary bank or credit union where you have direct deposits and history. These often approve via internal overrides and help anchor the cycle.
2. Predictable card issuers second
   - Issuers known for auto-approvals when profile cues

match. These are the cards that will reflect the mirror effect quickly.

3. Business funding third
   ○ If you are running both personal and business cycles, do business draws after initial personal approvals have posted or are in process. If your business bank is the same institution as your personal bank, you can do them adjacent.
4. Opportunistic fintechs and specialty lenders last
   ○ These can be more aggressive, but they also share data rapidly. Get them after you have some new limits showing, so they see prior approvals.

Why this order? Relationship lenders anchor trust. Predictable issuers give you new limits that create the mirror effect. Business funding adds separate capital. Opportunistic lenders then match or expand based on visible limits.

THE TIGHT WINDOW

Execute the applications within a 48- to 72-hour window when possible. Short window benefits:

- Hard inquiries do not all appear at once on bureau snapshots immediately. You lock in approvals before velocity looks bad.
- New accounts and limits take some time to report. If you have several approvals in the same window, downstream lenders see higher existing limits or approvals before the bureau shows all new entries.

Do not stretch the cycle over weeks. That invites EWS and other velocity checks.

THE MIRROR TECHNIQUE APPLIED

- When a new high limit posts on your file, lenders are more likely to match or exceed it.
- Use that by sequencing issuers that frequently underwrite higher limits second or third, so they see earlier approvals.
- Example flow: Relationship bank approval posts or shows as authorized pending. You hit issuer A and get a $15,000 approval. Issuer B sees the pending $15,000 and feels more comfortable offering $20,000.

Mirror works best when the approvals are visible to decisioning engines quickly. That is why the tight window matters.

BUSINESS + PERSONAL STACKING

Two major levers

1. Personal approvals.
2. Business approvals under the EIN.

If your business is established and has deposits, target business lines from lenders that underwrite on bank statements and do soft pull prequalification. Sequence business approvals after your core personal approvals, so combined reported limits create the mirror effect across both profiles.

Example outcome: Business side $60,000, personal side $70,000, total $130,000 available.

UTILIZATION AND DTI MANAGEMENT DURING THE CYCLE

- Immediately after approvals, do not max cards or take cash outs. High utilization flags automated models quickly.
- If initial approvals are lower than expected, consider asking for reconsideration only after waiting 7 to 21 days, and only when you can present stronger evidence, like direct deposit history or recently posted limits.
- Monitor DTI if lenders pull income and obligations. Avoid adding large installment debt simultaneously unless already planned.

BLACKLIST RISK CONTROL

- Do not open checking accounts with unknown banks in the days before a cycle. New deposit accounts can trigger ChexSystems reviews.
- Avoid P.O. boxes for business addresses. They show up as fraud signals in many fraud engines.
- If you have an EWS or ChexSystems flag, resolve it before attempting a stack. Relationship overrides can help, but you should not rely on them if you face shared blacklist flags.

IF AN APPLICATION GETS KICKED INTO MANUAL REVIEW

- Pause the cycle immediately. Stop applying until you know why. A manual review often means the system noticed a mismatch, and additional apps will increase suspicion.
- For manual review, respond with crisp documentation: pay stubs, bank statements, resolved balances. Keep communications concise and factual.
- Use your relationship bank to advocate. They can often escalate or vouch in ways a stranger cannot.
- If the problem is a fraud flag, address it with the sub-bureau directly and push for an error dispute while you halt further apps.

POST-CYCLE PLAY: SEASONING AND LEVERAGE

- Let new accounts report fully. Most issuers report within 30 to 45 days. During that time, maintain low utilization across lines.
- Use new credit strategically. You can request a limit increase after 60 to 120 days if usage and payments are clean. That compounds the mirror.
- If you received a mix of secured or small starter limits, use them responsibly and request upgrades in parallel months.

EXAMPLE CASE STUDY: THE 72-HOUR STACK

Profile

- Ella, score 710, utilization 6%, 10 tradelines, 5 years with local credit union. Small LLC deposits for 9 months.

Plan

- Day 0: Relationship credit union personal card application and small business line of credit pre-qual.
- Day 1: Target issuer A and issuer B personal cards back-to-back. Soft pre-qual checks earlier confirmed odds.
- Day 2: Business line formal application after receiving an indication from issuer A that approval is pending.
- All three submitted within 72 hours.

Result

- Credit union approves $10,000 personal line and fast-tracks business line to $40,000 based on deposits. Issuer A auto-approves $15,000. Issuer B approves $20,000. Total new capacity $85k in three days. Limits report within 30 days and creates further leverage for increases.

Key wins: relationship anchor, tight window, low utilization, business deposits visible.

THE FUNDING STACKING CHECKLIST

Pre-Cycle

- Pull reports and ChexSystems, dispute errors.
- Pay down utilization to target level 10% or lower.
- Align job title, address, phone across reports.
- Draft documentation for income and business activity.
- Prioritize bank list and confirm soft pull options.

Execution

- Execute applications in a 48- to 72-hour window.
- Start with relationship lenders, then predictable issuers, then business, then opportunistic entrants.
- Do not apply if any manual review is active. Pause and resolve.
- Monitor for instant feedback and be ready to produce docs fast.

Post-Cycle

- Keep utilization low while new limits season.
- Let accounts report 30 to 90 days before asking for increases.
- Use the mirror technique to request boosts from subsequent lenders.
- If a denial occurs, document the reason, fix, and reapply after fixes have had time to report.

FINAL NOTES AND WARNINGS

1. Stacking increases exposure. Always maintain a buffer for DTI and cash flow. Do not overextend because you can access capital.
2. Repeated cycles without seasoning raise flags. Space major stacking runs.
3. Some lenders share data quickly. The faster your approvals appear, the better. But if an issuer reports something odd, be prepared to address it quickly.
4. This system rewards discipline. The same habits that get you stacked will keep your funding sustainable long-term.

THE MINDSET OF A PRO STACKER

Funding stacking is a game of precision, not chance. Too many people hear about it, get excited, and start firing off applications like it's the lottery. That's how people trigger shutdowns, fraud flags, and end up blacklisted. The pros don't operate that way. They move like chess players: three, four, or five moves ahead.

Think Like the Bank

When you stack, don't ask, *"How much can I get?"* Instead, ask, *"What would the bank see if they looked at my file right now?"*

- Does your utilization look calm, not desperate?
- Does your employment and address history show stability?

- Are your new accounts spaced logically, or does it look like a grab for cash?

Banks love boring profiles. If your file looks clean, stable, and consistent, you look like a safe bet even if you're stacking aggressively in the background.

Momentum Is Everything

Funding stacking is like surfing. Once you catch a wave, you ride it until it carries you all the way in. That's why pros bundle applications within a short window. Momentum beats hesitation. Every approval you land becomes social proof for the next lender's algorithm.

If you drag it out, momentum dies. Inquiries start to pile up, new accounts hit your report, and the system starts asking questions.

Control Your Ego

There is a quiet threshold in funding where ambition turns into danger, and if you cross it without discipline, the system marks you in silence long before you ever see the consequences.

The easiest way to get burned is chasing vanity approvals. Don't stack just to say you landed a $25,000 line. Stack to build a foundation that multiplies over time. The game is cumulative. Ten thousand here, $15,000 there, another $20,000 on the business side, done right, you'll cross six figures quietly and sustainably.

The pros never get greedy. They play long-term.

Because in the shadows of the vault, the people who move quietly are the ones who survive, while the ones who chase applause always end up triggering alarms they never knew were there.

REAL-WORLD ILLUSTRATION (2025)

Amex Player:

Jasmine stacked her applications smartly, Amex first, Chase second, then her business credit union last. In 72 hours, she pulled $95,000 in combined approvals. She stopped there, even though she could have gone further. Why? She knew the next app would risk velocity flags.

And that restraint is what kept her invisible to the system, because the vault rewards strategy but punishes hunger every single time.

Velocity Victim:

Daniel heard about stacking and went wild, submitting apps at six different banks in the same week without preparation. His profile got flagged in EWS for suspicious activity. Instead of approvals, he got denials, and now he is locked out for twelve months.

And once the vault decides you are a risk, it does not knock, it does not warn, it simply closes the door and waits for you to learn a lesson the hard way.

Same credit scores. Same year. Different results. The difference wasn't the file; it was the mindset.

Because mindset is the invisible filter the system reads before anything else, and the ones who understand that truth are the ones who walk away with approvals, while everyone else walks away confused.

THE PRO STACKER'S RULEBOOK

1. **Move With Strategy, Not Emotion**: You plan the sequence, you don't improvise.
2. **Respect Seasoning**: New accounts need time before the next cycle. Don't rush.
3. **Don't Chase Every Card**: Focus on issuers that fit your blueprint, not every shiny offer.
4. **Quit While You're Ahead**: Walk away with clean approvals instead of pushing for one more and triggering flags.

If you take away one thing from this page, it's this: **funding stacking is a discipline, not a gamble.** When you play it like a professional, the system will reward you.

THE PRO STACKER'S QUICK SHEET

DO'S & DON'TS FOR FUNDING STACKING SUCCESS

DO's

- **Plan Ahead**
- Clean reports, align addresses, and lower utilization **before** stacking.
- **Use the Right Sequence**
- Relationship banks first → predictable issuers second → business funding third → opportunistic lenders last.

- **Move Fast**
- Keep the cycle tight—ideally 48 to 72 hours—so inquiries and new accounts don't derail approvals.
- **Mirror the Limits**
- Let high approvals feed into higher limits. Use the mirror effect strategically.
- **Leverage Both Sides**
- Combine personal + business funding for maximum capital.
- **Keep Utilization Low After Approval**
- Don't blow through new lines immediately. Show stability and let accounts season.
- **Document Everything**
- Have pay stubs, bank statements, and EIN docs ready in PDF format.

DON'Ts

- **Don't Go in Sloppy**
- High utilization, mismatched data, or recent derogatories kill approvals fast.
- **Don't Spray and Pray**
- Random apps at random banks = fraud alerts, velocity flags, and denials.
- **Don't Ignore Blacklists**
- ChexSystems, EWS, and internal bank lists matter. Clear them first.
- **Don't Get Greedy**
- Quit while you're ahead. One extra app can turn a clean sweep into a flagged profile.
- **Don't Neglect Seasoning**

- Let accounts age before running another cycle. Pros think in quarters, not weeks.
- **Don't Burn Bridges**
- Walking away from accounts in the red puts you on permanent internal blacklists.

QUICK REMINDER

Funding stacking is not gambling. It is a calculated, premeditated risk.

Every move is intentional. Every application is a chess piece.

Play the sequence correctly, and the approvals fall in your favor.

Rush the process, and the system closes before you ever reach the vault.

Stacking gets you in the door.

Understanding what waits behind it is what turns you into a real player.

TWELVE
THE ANTI-DECLINE CHECKLIST
STEP-BY-STEP: WHAT TO DO BEFORE APPLYING FOR ANY HIGH-LIMIT FUNDING

There is a moment right before you apply when the system quietly evaluates you, and if one detail is out of place, the vault decides your fate in silence long before you ever learn what went wrong.

Here's the truth: most denials don't come from bad credit; they come from sloppy preparation. The banks don't have time to figure you out. They scan, flag, and decide. If anything looks off, you're done before a human ever sees your file.

And once you understand how ruthless that first scan is, you realize the real danger isn't the denial itself but the invisible mark the system leaves when it decides you were not prepared to play.

That's why pros run through the Anti-Decline Checklist before every application cycle. Think of it like a pilot's pre-flight routine: tighten every bolt, check every gauge, then take off with confidence.

Because in the world behind the vault, only the people who prepare with precision ever make it through the turbulence without the system grounding them on sight.

STEP 1: CLEAN THE SURFACE

- **Credit Reports**: Pull all three (Experian, Equifax, TransUnion). Make sure there are no lingering errors, old addresses, or outdated employers.
- **Blacklist Reports**: Request your ChexSystems and Early Warning Services files. Clear anything small that could get flagged.
- **Sub-Bureaus**: Check LexisNexis, CoreLogic, and Innovis if you've had past denials. These "shadow bureaus" often trip people up.

STEP 2: FIX THE RATIOS

- **Utilization**: Keep revolving balances under 10% of your limits. Under 30% is the bare minimum.
- **Debt-to-Income (DTI)**: If your debt is too heavy relative to your reported income, you'll get choked at underwriting. Pay down or spread out balances before applying.

STEP 3: ALIGN THE STORY

- **Addresses**: Make sure your current address is consistent everywhere—reports, banking apps, and applications. No P.O. boxes unless absolutely necessary.

- **Employment**: List job titles that reflect stability and responsibility. "Supervisor" or "Manager" is stronger than "Walmart" alone.
- **Income**: Don't inflate beyond reason. AI cross-checks your reported number against averages for your occupation.

STEP 4: SEASON YOUR ACCOUNTS

- **New Tradelines**: Let new cards or loans season at least 60–90 days before stacking. Too fresh = instability.
- **Primary Accounts**: Keep checking and savings activity steady. Banks like to see regular deposits, not random spikes.

STEP 5: PREP DOCUMENTATION

- PDF bank statements (three to six months)
- Pay stubs or income proof
- EIN docs and business financials if going for business funding
- Clear ID (passport or driver's license, not expired)

Having these ready means that if your app goes into review, you can respond fast and confidently.

STEP 6: PLAN THE SEQUENCE

- Relationship banks first
- Predictable issuers second

- Business apps third
- Opportunistic lenders last

Order matters. Don't wing it—sequence your applications for maximum leverage.

STEP 7: RUN THE FINAL PRE-CHECK

Before you apply, ask yourself:

- *Is my utilization clean?*
- *Do my addresses and job info match across all reports?*
- *Have I cleared small balances or overdrafts?*
- *Is my income believable?*
- *Am I moving in a 48- to 72-hour window?*

If the answer isn't yes to all of the above, fix it before you hit "submit."

Case Study: The Checklist Saves the Day

Case: Jordan

Jordan had a 735 score and wanted to apply for a $20,000 card. Before pulling the trigger, he ran through the Anti-Decline Checklist. He realized his utilization was sitting at 38%. He paid down balances to under 9%, aligned his employer title from "Clerk" to "Assistant Manager," and cleared a $42 overdraft on an old checking account.

Result? Instant approval at $18,500. Without the checklist, he would have been flagged and denied.

KEY TAKEAWAY

Approvals don't go to the desperate; they go to the disciplined. If you want to avoid denials, don't play guesswork. Run the checklist every time. Because when the banks look at you, they're not just seeing your score; they're seeing your entire story. And if the story checks out, you're in.

And once you understand that the vault rewards the people who move with intention, every step you take becomes another line in a narrative the system cannot deny.

ANTI-DECLINE QUICK REFERENCE

Your Pre-Flight Checklist Before Every Application

STEP 1: CLEAN THE SURFACE

- Pull all three credit reports (Experian, Equifax, TransUnion)
- Check ChexSystems and Early Warning Services
- Verify LexisNexis, Innovis, and CoreLogic if you have had past denials
- Dispute errors and remove old addresses or employers

STEP 2: FIX THE RATIOS

- Revolving utilization under 10% (maximum 30%)
- Debt-to-income (DTI) in a healthy range
- Pay off small lingering balances

STEP 3: ALIGN THE STORY

- Address matches across all platforms
- Employer title listed as stable and responsible ("Supervisor" or "Manager" instead of "Clerk")
- Income believable and consistent with occupation averages

STEP 4: SEASON ACCOUNTS

- New tradelines aged 60-90 days
- Checking and savings deposits consistent with no unexplained spikes

STEP 5: PREP DOCUMENTATION

- Three to six months of bank statements in PDF format
- Pay stubs or income proof
- EIN documents and business financials if applying on the business side
- Valid, unexpired identification

STEP 6: PLAN THE SEQUENCE

- Relationship banks
- Predictable issuers
- Business applications
- Opportunistic lenders

STEP 7: FINAL PRE-CHECK

- Utilization clean
- No unresolved overdrafts or blacklist entries
- All information aligned across reports and documents
- Application cycle completed within 48 to 72 hours

Antoine Sallis Tip: If even one box is unchecked, don't hit "submit" yet. Fix it first. Approvals are earned in preparation, not in luck.

With this checklist in hand, you'll walk into every funding cycle positioned like a pro, and banks will see the story you *want* them to see.

THIRTEEN
LETTERS FROM THE INSIDE
REAL STORIES FROM BANKERS, UNDERWRITERS & WHISTLEBLOWERS

Sometimes the truth doesn't announce itself; it waits in the dark, watching, until you are finally ready to see what has been hiding behind the door.

If you've ever wondered what bankers and underwriters say behind closed doors, this is the chapter you've been waiting for. These aren't theories. These are letters from the inside, anonymous accounts, confessions, and whispered truths from people who have worked in the system and know how it really runs.

And once you hear the voices from the other side of the vault, the pieces you have been chasing finally fall into place, revealing a world that was never meant to be spoken out loud.

LETTER #1: THE BANKER'S CONFESSION

"Most people think we just look at credit scores and approve or deny. The truth? That's the last step. By the time I see your application, the system has already flagged you green, yellow, or red. If you're red, I

don't even get to argue for you. But if you're yellow, that's where I can step in. That's where relationships matter. I've approved people with 670 scores just because I've seen them keep steady deposits for five years. Meanwhile, I've denied 780s that looked unstable."

Lesson: You're not just a number. You're a file with a story—and bankers notice the story you're telling.

LETTER #2: THE UNDERWRITER'S NOTEBOOK

"We're trained to look for patterns. Too many new accounts in 90 days? Red flag. Address changes every six months? Red flag. Job-hopping every year? Red flag. The score doesn't erase those patterns. And here's something you'll never hear us admit: we know the credit bureaus make mistakes, but unless you bring it up and prove it, we take what's on the report as gospel. Don't assume we'll give you the benefit of the doubt."

Lesson: Consistency beats perfection. A stable, boring profile wins approvals over a flashy score with instability.

LETTER #3: THE WHISTLEBLOWER

"At my old bank, we had an internal list we called the 'do-not-touch file.' You could have perfect credit, but if you burned us once, including overdrafts, unpaid charge-offs, or suspicious activity, we blacklisted you forever. Most customers never knew why they were being denied. They'd just get a vague letter in the mail. Internally, we knew: once you were on the list, you weren't coming off."

Lesson: Protect your reputation with every institution you touch. One bad move can lock you out permanently, even if your credit score looks clean.

LETTER #4: THE CREDIT UNION INSIDER

"I've worked in a credit union for twelve years. We bend the rules more than the big banks, but we're still watching. Members who keep steady savings, take small loans and pay them off, and show up in person get special treatment. We'll push approvals through for them that we'd deny to strangers with higher scores. Why? Because loyalty matters. We're protecting the community, not just the balance sheet."

Lesson: Credit unions can be your secret weapon if you build a real relationship with them.

KEY TAKEAWAY

When you see funding from the inside, you realize the truth: approvals aren't just about credit scores. They are about the signals you send, the story your file tells, and the relationships you nurture. The insiders confirm what I have been telling you all along: it is not just math, but it is also trust.

And once you understand that trust is the invisible currency inside the vault, every move you make starts carrying the kind of weight the system cannot ignore.

THE AI GATEKEEPER

LETTER #5: THE DATA SCIENTIST'S PERSPECTIVE

"I worked on the machine learning models that score applicants behind the scenes. Here is what people do not realize: once the model has enough confidence, your fate is sealed before a human ever looks at your file. We build risk scores using hundreds of data points such as job stability, address history, payment velocity, and even how you type your application online. Do you know how many people get flagged because their IP address did not match their listed state? More than you would think. We are not trying to punish people; we are trying to predict risk, but the net is wide. If your data does not line up, the system errs on the side of 'deny.'"

Lesson: In 2025, AI is often the first and last word in funding. Consistency across every detail is no longer optional; it is survival.

LETTER #6: THE COMPLIANCE OFFICER

"I don't deny applications. I enforce rules. But what most customers don't realize is that compliance can override everything. If your file triggers a Bank Secrecy Act (BSA) or anti-money laundering (AML) flag, you're done. No banker, no underwriter, no manager can save you. We've had high-score applicants with spotless files denied because of large unexplained deposits or frequent transfers that looked like structuring. To us, safety outweighs profit. Once compliance flags you, there's no arguing."

Lesson: It's not always about your credit. Sometimes it's about *patterns that look risky* in the eyes of regulators. Always keep your banking activity transparent and explainable.

PAGE 2: THE HUMAN SIDE OF THE SYSTEM

LETTER #7: THE SENIOR UNDERWRITER

"I have been in the game for twenty years. What I will tell you is this: sometimes we just know when someone is playing the system. Multiple inquiries in the same week? We flag it. Applicants suddenly using new addresses? We flag it. But here is the twist: we also know when someone looks solid, even if their score is not high. I have pushed through 660 files with great consistency because stability speaks louder than numbers. And yes, sometimes we give the benefit of the doubt to people we know. Human judgment still exists, but you have to earn it."

Lesson: Underwriters may be bound by AI and scorecards, but relationships, stability, and narrative still allow the human element to shine through.

LETTER #8: THE FRIENDLY BANKER

"When I see a customer who treats the bank like a partner and not a tool, I go to bat for them. I have walked applications over to underwriting to push approvals through. But I only do it for people who have shown loyalty. The ones who maintain deposits, take our products, and show up in person. The drive-by customers chasing sign-up bonuses? We shut those down quickly. Loyalty is currency."

Lesson: Never underestimate the value of being seen as a partner. When bankers like you, they can bend the rules that AI and systems enforce.

EXPANDED KEY TAKEAWAY

From AI gatekeepers to compliance officers to bankers and underwriters, one thing is clear: the system is not just about numbers; it is about patterns, trust, and perception.

AI demands clean, consistent data.

Compliance demands explainable transactions.

Underwriters demand stability.

Bankers demand loyalty.

When you understand all four lenses, you stop playing defense. You build a profile that every part of the system wants to approve.

SUMMARY: THE INSIDER PLAYBOOK

After hearing straight from the bankers, underwriters, compliance officers, and even the data scientists building the AI, one truth stands tall: **the system is not simple. It's layered.** And if you want consistent approvals, you have to play the game on all levels at once.

1. AI'S PERSPECTIVE: CONSISTENCY IS KING

- Keep addresses, jobs, and income aligned across every system.
- Don't trigger velocity—too many apps or changes in too little time.
- Treat your file like it's being reviewed by a machine that never forgets.

2. COMPLIANCE'S PERSPECTIVE: TRANSPARENCY WINS

- Large, unexplained cash deposits = red flags.
- Frequent transfers between accounts = structuring risk.
- Play clean. Play explainable. Assume regulators are watching.

3. UNDERWRITER'S PERSPECTIVE: STABILITY OVER SCORE

- 670 with five years at the same job is greater than 780 with constant moves.
- Boring profiles are beautiful to underwriters.
- Don't chase perfection—chase predictability.

4. BANKER'S PERSPECTIVE: LOYALTY IS LEVERAGE

- Regular deposits, multiple products, and showing up in person matter.
- Bankers will go to bat for you if they see you as a partner, not a passerby.
- Loyalty buys exceptions that algorithms can't.

THE FOUR-DIMENSIONAL CHECKLIST

Before you apply, ask yourself:

1. **AI** – Does my data line up across the board?
2. **Compliance** – Would my banking activity raise eyebrows if regulators saw it?
3. **Underwriting** – Do I look stable, consistent, and low risk?
4. **Banking Relationship** – Have I invested enough in this institution for them to fight for me?

If you can check all four boxes, your odds of approval skyrocket. If you can't, you're walking into the system half-prepared—and that's where denials happen.

FINAL WORD

These letters were not just stories; they were confessions from the people who decide your financial fate.

They were the quiet truths spoken by the gatekeepers, the insiders, the unseen hands that approve, decline, or shadow your file without you ever knowing their names.

And once you read them closely, you feel the shift, the unsettling realization that the system has always had two languages, one for the public and one for the people on the inside.

When you see through their eyes, you realize something powerful:

The Great American Credit Secret is not just knowing how credit works; it is knowing how the system works.

It is understanding the currents beneath the surface, the patterns that shape decisions long before you apply, the silent rules that only insiders whisper about when the doors are closed and the lights are low.

Once you grasp that truth, you stop walking into the vault like a hopeful borrower and start moving like someone who understands the architecture of the system itself. You see the shadows behind the decisions, the invisible thresholds, the quiet risks, and the hidden opportunities waiting for the people who know how to read them.

And from that moment on, you are no longer just participating in the credit game; you are operating above it, navigating with the kind of confidence that only comes from knowing the secrets that were never meant for the public to see.

FOURTEEN
GRADUATION DAY
EVOLVING FROM BORROWER TO BANK-LEVEL PLAYER

Some doors only open for people who are willing to walk into the dark without knowing what waits on the other side, and that they just entered one of them. What comes next is not for spectators but for the ones who are ready to move like insiders instead of applicants.

Congratulations. If you have made it this far, you have already walked the halls of the vault. You have cracked the Credit Code, pulled back the curtain on underwriting, decoded the scorecards, and learned the blueprint for six-figure funding. You have seen the hidden triggers, the blacklist landmines, and even the insider letters straight from the people making the calls.

Now it is time for graduation.

This is not about being the smartest borrower in the room anymore. This is about becoming something different. This is about thinking like a bank-level player.

Because once you cross this line, the system stops being a mystery and starts becoming a map, and only the people who understand that shift ever make it to the other side of the vault.

WHY GRADUATION MATTERS

Most people never graduate. They stay stuck on the surface, chasing higher scores, chasing approvals, begging banks for credit like customers begging for service. But you? You are done with that. You are not just chasing approvals anymore; you are building leverage. *Graduation means stepping into a world most people never even realize exists, a world where the power shifts silently into your hands the moment you understand how to wield it.*

Graduation means flipping the game:

Instead of just being approved for funding, you decide how funding flows.

Instead of being subject to banks, you operate like one.

Instead of letting algorithms dictate your future, you build systems that reward you.

This is the moment where you stop reacting to the system and start shaping it around your intentions.

THE SHIFT IN MINDSET

Graduation is not about your score; it is about your perspective. Here is what separates borrowers from bankers:

Borrowers ask, "Will they approve me?"

Bank-Level Players ask, "How do I structure myself so they have no choice but to approve?"

Borrowers chase cards.

Bank-Level Players build relationships, leverage, and strategy.

Borrowers see credit as access.

Bank-Level Players see credit as currency.

Once that shift happens, every decision becomes a strategic move on a board most people do not even know they are standing on.

REAL-WORLD ILLUSTRATION

Borrower Mindset: Sarah, with a 780 score, applies randomly for a new card, gets denied, and feels powerless.

Bank-Level Mindset: Malik, with a 690 score, knows his stability, builds interbanking credit, and times his funding stack. He walks away with $100,000 in approvals while Sarah is still wondering why her perfect score was not enough.

Graduation is not about the number on your report; it is about playing the game at a higher level.

And the proof is simple: the system rewards the ones who understand its rhythm, not the ones who simply hope their numbers are enough.

THE CEREMONY

Consider this your ceremony. The tassel is turned. You have moved from the outside looking in to the inside looking out. You are not just a borrower anymore; you are stepping into the role of architect, strategist, and banker.

From here on out, every move you make with credit should be intentional, calculated, and structured like a professional. Because once you graduate, the stakes get higher, but so do the rewards.

And now that you stand on this side of the vault, you will see opportunities where others see obstacles, because you finally understand how the system thinks and how to make it work for you.

THE BORROWER VS. THE BANKER

The biggest leap you will make after graduation is mental. You have been conditioned to think like a borrower all your life: credit score chasing, approval begging, limit watching. Banks designed it that way. But when you flip your mindset, you realize the bank does not just lend; they leverage. *And once this truth finally sinks in, you begin to see the entire system with new eyes, noticing patterns, power shifts, and hidden mechanics that were invisible to you before.*

This is the moment where the game stops being a mystery and starts becoming a map, a map only insiders were ever meant to read.

Then you have learned The Great American Credit Secret.

Borrower's Reality:

- Begs for approvals
- Accepts whatever limit they're given
- Thinks a 780 score guarantees success
- Believes banks hold all the power

Bank-Level Player's Reality:

- Structures a file that *forces* approvals
- Uses one limit to unlock the next (mirror effect)
- Leverages relationships for overrides
- Understands banks need borrowers to survive

The day you realize **banks need you just as much as you need them** is the day you graduate.

PAGE 3: THE THREE PILLARS OF BANK-LEVEL THINKING

To play at the bank's level, you have to master three pillars: **Structure, Leverage, and Multiplication.**

1. STRUCTURE

- Build a profile that looks bulletproof: stability, consistency, and aged tradelines.
- Keep your utilization low and your reports clean.
- Align your story: job, income, address, accounts.

2. LEVERAGE

- Use approvals strategically to stack into higher limits.
- Tap both personal and business credit for maximum funding.
- Borrow at low interest, invest in high-return assets.

3. MULTIPLICATION

- Don't just borrow—make the borrowed money work.
- Turn credit into cash flow: real estate, businesses, investments.
- Let your new income streams fuel stronger banking relationships, which lead to more approvals.

That's the cycle banks play every single day. When you graduate, you start playing it too.

PAGE 4: THE EVOLUTION PATH – FROM BORROWER TO LENDER

Here's the roadmap for evolving step by step:

1. **Survival Mode (Borrower Mindset)**
   - Focused only on getting approved.
   - Score-driven, not structure-driven.
   - Feels powerless when denied.
2. **Strategic Borrower (Stacker Mindset)**
   - Learns to sequence apps, manage utilization, and play the mirror effect.
   - Wins funding cycles of $50,000–$100,000.
   - Starts to feel like the system is predictable.
3. **Bank-Level Player (Graduation)**
   - Leverages both personal + business credit.
   - Builds interbanking credit with consistent deposits.
   - Uses credit as a tool to multiply assets.
4. **Lender Mindset (Mastery)**
   - Stops asking for credit—starts offering it.

- Uses capital to fund businesses, joint ventures, even other people's opportunities.
- Positions themselves like the bank, where money flows through them instead of to them.

PAGE 5: CASE STUDY – THE GRADUATE IN ACTION

Case: Andre

Andre started, like most borrowers, score-focused. He had a 720 but was frustrated with $5,000 to $7,000 limits. After learning the stacking game, he built a structure and went into a cycle: $70,000 personal, $50,000 business. Instead of blowing it on expenses, he used $30,000 to acquire a vending machine business with twelve locations.

The business brought in $8,000 a month in cash flow. Within six months, Andre had stable deposits, stronger interbanking credit, and bank officers calling him with new offers. The very same banks that once gave him $5,000 were now offering lines of $50,000 because they saw him operating like a business, not just a borrower.

Andre did not just get approvals; he **graduated**.

PAGE 6: THE BANK-LEVEL MINDSET IN 2025

Graduation in 2025 means understanding this:

- AI runs the numbers.
- Compliance enforces the rules.
- Underwriters check stability.
- Bankers reward loyalty.

The graduate plays all four layers at once. They know their file is AI-friendly, compliance-clean, underwriter-stable, and banker-approved. That's why they never fear denials—they move with certainty.

When you walk into a bank with this mindset, you stop asking, *"Will they approve me?"* and start asking, *"How much capital do I want to deploy right now?"*

That's the day you stop being a borrower and start being the bank.

AFTERTHOUGHT: THE GRADUATE'S VISION

Graduation is not just a chapter; it is a crossing over. You came into this book thinking about credit as something you chase, a number you protect, an approval you hope for. Now you understand that credit is leverage, credit is trust, and credit is power. *Once your mindset shifts, you begin to see the system from a height you never knew existed, a vantage point reserved only for the ones who understand how the vault really thinks.*

Banks are no longer towers you look up at. They are chessboards you can navigate. Algorithms are no longer mysteries, they are formulas you can game. Underwriters are not gatekeepers, they are people who read the story you write. And relationships? Those are your secret passages through walls most people do not even know exist. *When you move with this awareness, the entire financial world starts responding to you differently, as if you stepped onto a path only insiders have ever walked.*

THE FUTURE YOU'RE WALKING INTO

Picture yourself a year from now:

- You walk into a bank meeting, not nervous, but prepared.
- You don't beg for approvals—you present a case so tight they can't say no.
- You don't chase credit cards—you decide which institutions deserve your deposits, your loyalty, your business.
- You don't fear denials—because you know how to reset, realign, and come back stronger.

And here's the real kicker: you don't just use credit for survival— you use it for expansion. Businesses. Assets. Investments. You don't live in the system anymore—you build through it.

A FINAL CHALLENGE

Most people will never graduate. They will stay stuck in borrower mode, chasing high scores, wondering why denials hit them, never realizing the deeper system at play. But not you. *You have stepped into a realm most people never even glimpse, a space where the mechanics behind the curtain finally come into focus, and the entire credit world rearranges itself around your understanding.*

You have got the insider playbook. You have got the checklists, the scorecards, the mindset shifts. You have walked through every chapter and seen the vault from the inside out. Now the question is simple:

Will you act like the graduate, or will you slip back into the crowd?

Because once you have seen how the machine truly works, going back to the surface is not just a mistake, it is a loss of the power you have earned.

CLOSING THOUGHT

The tassel has turned. The ceremony is over. The world beyond the borrower's mindset is open to you. From this day forward, stop asking, "Can I get approved?" and start asking, "What will I build with the approvals I control?"

That single shift in thought is the dividing line between those who borrow and those who leverage, between those who hope for opportunities and those who create them.

Because the real Great American Credit Secret is not about access; it is about power. And today, graduate, that power is in your hands.

Once you recognize that truth, the entire financial landscape becomes a set of tools waiting for the person bold enough to use them.

With your graduation complete, we step into the final stretch, the conclusion of this journey. But before we close the book, there is one more set of tools you will need: the strategies that transform knowledge into action and help you use credit like a banker, not just think like one.

And when you master those final tools, the vault does not just open for you; it stays open.

FIFTEEN

THE REAL-WORLD PLAYBOOK
USING CREDIT LIKE A
BANKER IN EVERYDAY LIFE

Graduation is the ceremony. The real world is the test.

The question is, now that you are thinking like a bank-level player, how do you apply that mindset every single day? *Because once you cross this threshold, the system starts watching you differently, waiting to see whether you rise to the level you just unlocked or crumble under the weight of the power you now possess.*

This chapter is about shifting from knowledge to application, taking the theory, the checklists, the insider secrets, and building a daily rhythm that keeps you winning approvals, stacking funding, and multiplying wealth. *It is the moment where your newfound identity meets the real world, and you discover that mastery is not a concept; it is a habit formed in the shadows long before the vault ever opens again.*

THE BANK-LEVEL DAILY OPERATING SYSTEM

1. PROTECT THE PROFILE LIKE IT'S CURRENCY

- Every transaction you make is part of your story.
- Don't swipe recklessly—spend in a way that builds trust with issuers.
- Pay balances before they report. A clean utilization cycle makes you look unstoppable.

2. BUILD BANKING LOYALTY EVERY MONTH

- Auto-transfer to savings to show discipline.
- Keep deposits steady—banks reward predictability.
- Rotate use of credit cards so every issuer sees activity and gets their "slice" of loyalty.

3. THINK LIKE A CAPITAL MANAGER, NOT A CUSTOMER

- Don't ask, *"Can I afford this?"* Ask, "What's the return on deploying this credit?"
- Every swipe should be strategic—travel points, cashback, business leverage.
- Keep personal spending lean so you can funnel approvals into assets that multiply.

THE "BANKER'S EYE" IN 2025

Here's the trick: bankers look for two things—**risk** and **potential.**

When you look at your own file through that lens, you can spot what they see before they do:

- Too many recent apps = risk.
- High utilization = risk.
- Long job history, strong deposits = potential.
- Consistency in addresses, accounts, and payments = potential.

If you can spot risks and clean them before an application, you'll always look like potential.

Real-World Case Study: The Post-Grad Move

Case: Alicia

After graduating, Alicia stopped thinking like a borrower. She structured her file clean, stacked $90,000 in approvals, and didn't waste it. Instead, she put $25,000 into e-commerce inventory, $15,000 into marketing, and $10,000 into a credit-builder trade-line that boosted her limits further. Within six months, she had tripled her monthly income.

Banks that once gave her $5,000 were now offering $30,000 without her even applying. Why? Because Alicia wasn't playing the borrower's game anymore. She was playing the banker's game —deploying credit as leverage, not survival.

THE REAL-WORLD PLAYBOOK CHECKLIST

Before every funding move, ask yourself (*Because the system evaluates you in silence long before any decision appears on the screen*):

- **Is my file AI-friendly** (clean, consistent, low utilization)?
- *If the algorithm senses disorder, it quietly shuts the door before a human ever reviews your name.*
- **Is my activity compliance clean** (no unexplained spikes or questionable transfers)?
- *Compliance officers look for irregular patterns, and even a single odd movement can trigger a hidden flag.*
- **Is my history underwriter stable** (addresses, job history, tradelines)?
- *Underwriters read your profile like a story, and any inconsistency makes them assume something is hiding in the gaps.*
- **Is my loyalty banker approved** (steady deposits, multiple products, consistent activity)?
- *Bankers advocate for the clients who treat the institution like a financial home, not a temporary stop.*

If you can say yes to all four, you're no longer walking into the vault as a borrower. You're walking in as a partner.

AFTERTHOUGHT: YOUR NEW NORMAL

Once you graduate, the biggest challenge is not getting approved; it is staying disciplined. The temptation will always be there to fall back into borrower mode, to chase cards just to flex limits, or to treat approvals like free money. Do not. *Because the moment you slip, the system notices, and the vault that once opened for you can just as easily start to close again, watching to see if you prove worthy of the power you were given.*

Your new normal is structure. Your new normal is leverage. Your new normal is multiplication.

This is the identity shift the average person never reaches, the point where credit stops being a tool and becomes a weapon in skilled hands.

Because from this point forward, you are not a student anymore. You are a bank-level player. And the vault? It is no longer locked; you have the keys. *What you unlock with those keys will define the next chapter of your life.*

FINAL CHAPTER: THE LEGACY OF THE GREAT AMERICAN CREDIT SECRET

CARRYING THE TORCH INTO THE FUTURE

You have now walked through all three volumes of this journey:

Part 1 taught you the foundation, the mechanics of credit, and the blueprint for building it.

Part 2: In the Age of AI showed you the new frontier, how artificial intelligence is rewriting the rules, and how to adapt before the world catches on.

Part 3: Inside the Bank took you past the velvet rope and deep into the vault, revealing what banks, underwriters, compliance officers, and even AI systems really see when they look at you.

And now, you have graduated.

This is not the end; it is the start. Because knowledge without action is useless. A secret unshared dies. But when you apply it, when you live it, when you teach it, you carry **The Great American Credit Secret** forward.

You become part of the underground lineage of people who understand how the system works, not how it appears to work.

THE VISION: BUILDING YOUR LEGACY

Imagine five years from now.

You are not stressing over approvals anymore. You are orchestrating funding cycles with precision. You are not just borrowing, you are deploying capital into assets that pay you month after month. You have flipped the game.

The world around you begins to shift as you move with the calm confidence of someone who understands exactly how to pull the levers everyone else fears touching.

Your family looks at you differently. Your community leans on you for guidance. People wonder how you always seem to figure it out. What they do not know is that you have mastered a playbook that was hidden in plain sight.

You are not just fixing credit, you are fixing futures. You are not just getting approved, you are building empires.

This is the legacy of The Great American Credit Secret.

And now that you carry it, the only question left is what you will build with the power in your hands.

THE ACTION PLAN: YOUR NEXT MOVES

Here's how to take this knowledge and make it your new reality:

1. **Audit Your File**
   - Pull all reports: Experian, Equifax, TransUnion

- Dispute and fix errors. Clean the surface. Add tradelines

2. **Stabilize Your Story**
   - Align your job title, income, and address everywhere.
   - Pay down utilization to under 10%.
   - Let new accounts season 60–90 days.

3. **Run Your First Funding Stack**
   - Sequence: Relationship banks → Predictable issuers → Business → Opportunistic lenders.
   - Execute within 48–72 hours.
   - Track approvals, denials, and seasoning for your next cycle. Then repeat in six months.

4. **Multiply, Don't Consume**
   - Use funding for assets—businesses, real estate, and credit products that build income.
   - Avoid treating approvals like a lottery win.

5. **Play the Long Game**
   - Build loyalty with banks and credit unions.
   - Use the mirror effect to climb into six figures.
   - Run clean cycles once or twice a year, not recklessly.

6. **Teach Someone Else**
   - Share the knowledge. Mentor a family member, friend, or peer.
   - The legacy of this secret grows when you pass it on.

FINAL WORD

The book closes. The vault hums. Your power expands.

This is the moment you step into a world where leverage is deliberate, trust is earned, and credit becomes a weapon that builds empires.

This is your final page, but it is only your first move.

The Great American Credit Secret was never about scores or limits. It was about stepping into the shadows behind the system and learning to see what the world never taught you to notice. It was about discovering that credit is not a number but a language, a power source, a quiet intelligence that only reveals itself to the people who know where to look. And somewhere along this journey, you became one of those people.

For years, the banks held the script, and everyone else recited lines without ever understanding the play. But you crossed a threshold. You saw the machinery. You watched how decisions are made in silence, how trust is measured in patterns, and how leverage belongs to those who master it, not those who hope for it.

There is a thrill in that, a kind of quiet joy that feels almost forbidden, like finding a door that was never meant to open for you but did anyway.

Now the final question rises before you, steady and profound: What will you build with this power?

Because the bank is not a counter, not a logo, not a building of stone and glass. It is a way of thinking. A way of moving. A way of shaping your financial world with intention instead of fear. And now, graduate, that way of thinking belongs entirely to you.

You are no longer outside looking in. You carry the vault within you.

So let the curtain fall. Let the lights dim. Let the journey settle into memory. The trilogy closes, but your power does not. What you choose to create next will become your legacy, your proof that the knowledge you gained here did not end on the page.

And now, as the final door closes behind you, one truth remains, quiet and absolute.

This is:

The Great American Credit Secret.